EVEN MORE

HACKING
ENGAGEMENT

New
Ways

to Make Learning Fun
for All Students

HACK™
Learning
SERIES

JAMES ALAN
STURTEVANT

TIMES
TEN

Even More Hacking Engagement
© 2023 by Times 10 Publications
Highland Heights, OH 44143 USA
Website: 10publications.com

All web links in this book are correct as of the publication date but may have become inactive or otherwise modified since that time.

Cover and Interior Design by Steven Plummer
Editing by Jordan Young
Copyediting by Jennifer Jas
Project Management by Jen Z. Marshall

Paperback ISBN: 978-1-956512-33-5
eBook ISBN: 978-1-956512-34-2
Hardcover ISBN: 978-1-956512-35-9

Library of Congress Cataloging-in-Publication Data is available for this title.

First Printing: February 2023

I've been married to Penny Sturtevant for over three decades. She's my romantic, supportive, and intellectual companion. This book is dedicated to her.

CONTENTS

Introduction 7

Hack 101: Sign the Magna Carta 9

Hack 102: Embody Maslow 13

Hack 103: Create a Script 17

Hack 104: Learn Something Special about Each Student 21

Hack 105: Generate Leads 25

Hack 106: Manifest a Vision 29

Hack 107: Amplify Empathy 33

Hack 108: Ask the Experts 37

Hack 109: Pass the Dinner Table Test 41

Hack 110: Clear the Higher-Level-Thinking Bar 45

Hack 111: Collaborate on a Virtual Landing Pad 49

Hack 112: Give the Gift of GIFs 53

Hack 113: Champion Self-Assessment 57

Hack 114: Fire Up the Random Name Generator 61

Hack 115: Find the Flow 65

Hack 116: Display Some Bling 69

Hack 117: Stage a Haiku Slam 73

Hack 118: Inspire Ambitious Goals 77

Hack 119: Conduct a Negative Thought Experiment 81

Hack 120: Meet Me in the Agora 85

Hack 121: Define Your Teaching 89

Hack 122: Deputize Devil's Advocates 93

Hack 123: Reconsider Wikipedia 97

Hack 124: Initiate Ostentatious Reward Day 101

Hack 125: Embark on a Formative Journey 105

Hack 126: Flip a Podcast 109

Hack 127: Promote a Process 113

Hack 128: Explore an Interactive Timeline. 117

Hack 129: Leverage a Learning Experience 121

Hack 130: Manifest a Room Full of Cohorts 125

Hack 131: Hone Your Nonverbal Presentation Skills 129

Hack 132: Eliminate Gaps 133

Hack 133: Get Them to Draw Again 137

Hack 134: Transform a Rubric 141

Hack 135: Make Assessment Engaging 145

Hack 136: Create Clarity 149

Hack 137: Look Fly on Friday 153

Hack 138: Promote Brand Ambassadors. 157

Hack 139: Stop Cross-Examining Your Students. 161

Hack 140: Insert Your Talking Head. 165

Hack 141: Leverage a Bit of Self-Deprecation. 169

Hack 142: Form Hook Production Teams 173

Hack 143: Engage All Five Senses 177

Hack 144: Scamper Through Your Next Evaluation. 181

Hack 145: Embrace Anonymity 185

Hack 146: Tease Out Relevancy 189

Hack 147: Empathetically Expose Bias 193

Hack 148: Foster Functionality. 197

Hack 149: Move, People! 201

Hack 150: Start Having Fun Again 205

Conclusion 209

Sneak Peek: *Dear Math: Why Kids Hate Math and
What Teachers Can Do About It*. 213

About the Author. 219

More from Times 10 Publications. 221

Resources from Times 10 Publications. 225

INTRODUCTION

STILL LOVE THE music from my era. I have all my favorite R&B hits from the 1970s, '80s, and '90s on my *Dad's Party Jamz* playlist on my Spotify account. My *Dinner Tracks* playlist contains smooth jazz favorites that provide excellent background music when we break bread with friends and family. I became even more of a Spotify disciple once I learned how to use the *Enhance* feature. When you activate this magnificent tool, your playlist populates with song suggestions. These new options are based on the music preferences you've already expressed through your usage. I still love all my old jamz, but it's always great to hear new choices. Each of my Spotify playlists has significantly grown thanks to *Enhance*. I haven't gotten rid of the great old stuff; I've just added great new stuff.

Think of this book as hitting the *Enhance* button on your *Student Engagement* playlist. I wrote *Hacking Engagement* and *Hacking Engagement Again* in 2016 and 2017, respectively. I love the content in those books, and I use Hacks from each one every time I step in front of young people. Since I wrote my last Hack back in 2017, I've been exposed to, or I've created, so many impactful new ideas that I simply must share. I'm closing in on my fourth decade in teaching. Rarely does a week go by that I don't find myself chomping at the bit the night before class because I'm excited to give a new idea a try. I'm excited to share fifty new ideas with you in *Even More Hacking Engagement*.

When you launch the Hacks in this book, the enjoyment level of your students will spike. Learning can be fun, and as a marvelous dividend on your investment, your personal enjoyment of teaching will spike as well. You'll be excited to get to school and try a new Hack. Now, let's enhance your *Student Engagement* playlist!

SIGN THE MAGNA CARTA

THE PROBLEM: TEACHERS RARELY INVOLVE STUDENTS IN CREATING CLASSROOM PROCEDURES

THIS HACK PROVIDES a magnificent idea for the first day of school, and you can also apply it to other junctures on the calendar. It's never too late to address classroom management issues and revisit classroom procedures; I've done it as late as April.

I live in Ohio, a truly garden-variety state. If it's in our teacher rubric, it's probably in yours. This directive comes from the *Ohio Teacher Evaluation Rubric* under the domain *Classroom Environment*. Here's what it takes to score "accomplished" on the rubric:

> *The teacher and students have collaboratively estab-lished consistent use of routines, procedures, and transi-tions that are effective in maximizing instructional time. On-task behavior is evident and ensured by students. Students initiate responsibility for effective operation of the classroom.*

Congratulations, Ohio! This is a great objective, and it's often overlooked. Now, let's ace this rubric!

THE HACK: CHALLENGE STUDENTS TO FORM A CONSENSUS ON CLASSROOM PROCEDURES

The Magna Carta was signed by King John of England in 1215. By doing so, his absolute powers were then limited, and England was no longer an absolute monarchy. Since then, the United Kingdom has been a beacon of good government. Let's make our classrooms high-functioning and humane learning environments—beacons of great classroom management in our schools and districts. This *Magna Carta* jigsaw activity is a perfect way to help achieve this noble objective.

Your first task is to decide which rules or classroom procedures you'd like students to debate. For the college courses I taught last semester, we came up with four major classroom management topics:

- Attendance

- Late submissions

- Summative assessment revision

- Cell phone use

Break your class into groups that will debate the management topics you've selected. Groups must have at least as many members as there are topics. I made certain that each group had at least four members. If a group has more, then a few students get to partner up. Once they are in their debate groups, they number off from one to four. Each group then has at least one resident expert:

1. All the ones focused on attendance.

2. All the twos focused on late submissions.

3. All the threes focused on summative assessment revision.

4. All the fours focused on cell phone use.

As with all jigsaws, students then leave their debate groups and congregate with those who share the same topic number—their newly formed topic groups. Prior to class, I formulated rational opposing positions on each topic, making certain that I only offered policy options I could live with (this is not anarchy). In their topic groups, students discuss the implications of each position. They do not need to come to a consensus but just discuss. When they return to their debate groups, they are deemed experts on their topic. Then, the debate groups navigate each topic and try to come to a consensus on each.

After a period of debate, the class reconvenes and each group is prompted about their conclusions on each topic. If you have an even number of debate groups and most of those groups have an even number of members, your potential for deadlock is high. In that case, you become the tiebreaker, just like the vice president in the US Senate.

The final step is the signing of the Magna Carta. You may want to use an online form to present the classroom decisions on each topic. Students can comply or dissent and even compose a narrative explaining their dissent. See Image 101 for an example of a class consensus on Google Forms.

Dilemma 3: Assessment Revisions *

○ Agree

○ Disagree

I disagree with the consensus on Dilemma 3. I'll explain my reasons below.

Long answer text

Image 101: An example of a class consensus form.

When I review the form, I am supplied with ample information about which students may struggle with which policies. This is superb intel before I am forced to learn this information in confrontational ways. Armed with this valuable knowledge, I go to work helping dissenters cope and perhaps even coaxing them to buy-in status so we end up with an agreement that everyone signs.

WHAT YOU CAN DO TOMORROW

- **Read your state's teacher standards for the classroom environment.** It may be similar to my example from Ohio.

- **Create a list of important classroom management topics.** Keep this list short and include just the major issues.

- **Create rational sides to classroom procedures topics.** Make sure you can live with the options.

Before you move on to the next Hack, reread the *Ohio Teacher Evaluation Rubric* passage. This activity checks all the boxes. Student consensus on classroom procedures will help to create an engaging classroom environment.

EMBODY MASLOW

THE PROBLEM: SOME STUDENTS LACK EMPATHY FOR PEERS

GREW UP IN a small college town in Southeastern Ohio. Both my town and my school were homogeneous. Not only did my classmates look alike, but they also mostly thought and acted alike.

My father was a professor at the local college, and in my sophomore year of high school, he was awarded a sabbatical at the University of Hawaii. So, we packed up and moved to an island for a year. Our family lived on the University of Hawaii campus, and I attended a large urban Honolulu high school. It was an eye-opening experience because I was one of just a few white kids at the school. My classmates often called me *Haole*. This derogatory label applies to a foreigner, an outsider, or one who is different.

My objective that year was to keep a low profile. I didn't like being called *Haole*, but I tolerated it. I was friendly with my classmates but in subtle ways. I deemed it safer to curtail my outgoing nature. I got through the year okay, but I was a different kid than in my past school experiences—I was quiet and not willing to stand out. When I became a teacher, this experience inspired deep empathy for my students who may feel different from most of their classmates. These differences may be based on culture, ethnicity, religion, sexual orientation, or even creed.

You have students who feel different. Maybe they aren't being authentic as a result. Abraham Maslow is here to help.

THE HACK: TEACH EMPATHY WITH MASLOW'S HIERARCHY OF NEEDS

Let's leverage Abraham Maslow's powerful ideas. This venerable education thinker promoted his *hierarchy of needs* many decades ago, and it's still remarkably relevant. His ideas are typically illustrated as a pyramidal template. Here's a refresher:

- Fifth level: Self-Actualization

- Fourth level: Esteem

- Third level: Love and Belonging

- Second level: Safety

- First level: Physiological (food and clothes)

> *Challenge kids to elect five empathy leaders.*

This idea came from the book *Anxious* by Christine Ravesi-Weinstein. Conduct a brief, direct instruction session where you give students an illustration of Maslow's template pyramid and then describe each level. Also, explore the idea of empathy and what it means to your students. Encourage them to share about times when they had to understand a different perspective. Once students can describe Maslow's hierarchy (at least in a basic one-or-two-sentence way) and define the word empathy, your class is all set to role-play.

Challenge kids to elect five empathy leaders. These are students who peers believe best embody this noble concept. Once you have five empathy leaders, number them off from one to five in any way you see fit. The number they're assigned will coincide with a Maslow hierarchy level. For example, the empathy leader with number three is responsible for Love and Belonging. Organize the rest of the students by numbering them off from one to five. Once kids have their numbers, they join their empathy leader with the same number, and they're ready for your prompt.

Share this prompt with all five groups:

> *Dramatize two classroom scenarios. One where a student feels at home in your assigned Maslow level, and one where they do not.*

Give them no other instructions, and give them just five minutes to come up with their two productions. After the performances, prompt the entire class to list ways that peers can help one another climb Maslow's pyramid.

WHAT YOU CAN DO TOMORROW

- **Conduct a Maslow refresher.** Familiarize yourself with Maslow's hierarchy by downloading a basic PDF.
- **Create a brief, direct instruction presentation on Maslow's hierarchy and the concept of empathy.** Share the PDF and then briefly talk about it. Don't get into examples or talk about personal experiences. That's for the students to demonstrate. Do the same with empathy. You may also include a short formative assessment to make sure they have it. Take no more than five minutes for this step.
- **Create an online Form Exit Ticket for students to share personal struggles that this activity may**

have inspired them to consider. This can take place after the debriefing. This activity may be transformational and an opportunity for you and your students to learn valuable information.

We want all students to be at the top of Maslow's pyramid so they will feel connected and engaged with their learning. Facilitating an empathetic classroom will be a huge help.

CREATE A SCRIPT

THE PROBLEM: A STAGNANT CLASSROOM UNDERMINES STUDENT ENGAGEMENT

'VE HAD A handful of overconfident education undergrads inform me that they weren't too worried about their future classroom management. Yet they should be. Classroom management is harder than it looks on TV sitcoms. I found it hard, and I'm one who always got excellent evaluations. Consequently, in the Education classes I now teach, we focus on creating a spectacular learning culture where classroom management problems are minimized. We research it, discuss it, speculate about it, and role-play about it, and yet, nothing fully prepares a young teacher for what they will face once it's showtime.

I wasn't prepared when I became a teacher in the late summer of 1985. It was a different world, and direct instruction absolutely dominated the airwaves. This statement may aggravate those who are dedicated to nostalgia, but student boredom was rampant. How would you like to sit through seven periods of direct instruction every day? Today, we engage students markedly better.

George Perry was my principal, and he gave me the chance of a lifetime by hiring me. (Thank you, Mr. Perry!) But I also want to thank George for a gift he gave me—a gift that benefited decades worth of my students. I've shared it with hundreds of future teachers, and it's hard to calculate just how many kids have been engaged and will be engaged by this gift. Mr. Perry was pleased with my performance as a rookie, but he accurately sensed that, like most newbies, I struggled with classroom management. Okay, enough buildup. Here's what George said to me:

> *The greatest classroom management tool is a well-organized lesson plan.*

This directive was not only solid in terms of classroom management, but it has also proven to be a gateway to student engagement.

THE HACK: EACH DAY, CREATE A ONE-PAGE SCRIPT FOR YOUR INSTRUCTION

For each day of teaching, create a script to keep the class on track. Show each instructional event and their start times. See Image 103 for an example of my script for the *Magna Carta* lesson in Hack 101. The class time was from 12:00 to 12:50.

341 Day 1 Script

Learning Target	12:00
Intro Slides	12:05
*Padlet Profile Pic	
*Week 1 HyperDoc	
*Cohort List	
Magna Carta Slides	12:20
*Ridiculous Rule IdeaBoard	
The Magna Carta	12:40
The Exit Ticket	12:45

*Activities that can be sacrificed

Image 103: My classroom script for a class from 12:00 to 12:50.

Note that the document includes nine underlined links. Before class begins, I open all links and project them on my screen. Granted, it makes for a lot of open windows, but the organizational trade-off and instant access make it worth it. If you're an early education teacher, your schedule looks different than a middle school or high school teacher. But please consider adapting this idea to fit your circumstances.

This method promotes engagement because you can sacrifice certain activities if time demands or if you sense that engagement is lagging. In this example, the ultra-engaging *Magna Carta* activity is the focus of the lesson. All other activities must work around it—it's the centerpiece. Before class, I print a hard copy of my script to keep myself on track. I also print an additional copy for a trusted student, deputizing them to hold their teacher accountable. You'll be amazed at how such a tactic will also help with any classroom management issues you're experiencing.

WHAT YOU CAN DO TOMORROW

- **Determine the central engagement activity for your lesson.** What is the key activity students will do—the heart of the day? Put this on your script first and then build around it.

- **Create an online doc that lists each instructional event for the lesson.** After you've built this list, insert hyperlinks. For example, a link to a slideshow presentation that contains a learning target.

- **Designate times for each major event to begin.** This is a crucial step. You want to start each activity at the designated time. This is the magic of staying on track.

- **Print a hard copy.** This serves as my old-school road map. You can check off activities as they're completed or skip activities deemed less important if time gets crunched.
- **Deputize a student.** This is a wonderful tactic to help you bond with a kid. Perhaps deputize a student with whom you desperately need a stronger bond.

My former principal George Perry passed away a number of years ago, and I'm happy to report that his spirit and impact live on. Thanks again, Mr. Perry.

104

LEARN SOMETHING SPECIAL ABOUT EACH STUDENT

THE PROBLEM: IT'S HARD TO ENGAGE KIDS IF YOU DON'T KNOW THEM

BONDING WITH STUDENTS is a big deal, and it's the glue that makes student engagement Hacks stick. In a 2019 article in *Education Week*, Sarah Sparks argues:

A Review of Educational Research analysis of 46 studies found that strong teacher-student relationships were associated in both the short- and long-term with improvements on practically every measure schools care about.

Sparks wrote these words pre-COVID. We all know how much the pandemic profoundly impacted our students. Many kids (and adults) are struggling academically, socially, and emotionally. What was true in 2019 is doubly true today: students need us.

"Strong" student-teacher relationships are a key part of creating an exceptional classroom culture. Such an environment is fertile ground for learning and student engagement. Engaging all your students is a supreme challenge, but the logical first step is to forge a bond with each of your kids.

THE HACK: PLAY A GUESSING GAME ABOUT STUDENTS

Start your bonding quest by prompting students to unveil something about themselves that others probably don't know and that they are willing to share. Ask them to post their secret anonymously on a virtual bulletin board like *Padlet* or *IdeaBoardz*. These are two easily utilized platforms where all the student submissions will be clearly visible to the class. After the students have posted their secrets, go from post to post and encourage students to guess who authored each.

Prompt them to keep guessing until someone hits paydirt. Once the culprit is successfully identified, have them stand and offer any additional information about why they posted the fact and anything else they wish to add. Ask them to continue standing, thus making the next unveiling easier with one less option. Continue until all students are standing. You will learn a lot about your kids, and they will learn a lot about one another. Who knew that the demure, petite female in the back row was just months away from becoming a black belt and that the starting quarterback who sits up front dreams of one day becoming a sommelier?

WHAT YOU CAN DO TOMORROW

- **Evaluate virtual bulletin boards.** Padlet and IdeaBoardz are great tools for public posting activities. Whatever you use, make certain the posts are legible to all your students.

- **Keep track of who posted what.** This is awesome information you can utilize, but only if you remember it. Record the information on the Padlet before you delete the posts.

- **Schedule another round.** Kids rapidly evolve and have more interesting facts to share beyond one round. This can be an outstanding icebreaker at the beginning of each nine weeks.

Learning interesting and special facts about the citizens of your class is an important bonding gateway.

GENERATE LEADS

THE PROBLEM: MANY EDUCATORS RELEGATE BONDING EFFORTS ONLY TO THE EARLY PART OF THE SEMESTER

RECENTLY PUT TOGETHER a cabinet from IKEA for my daughter-in-law. When I removed everything from the box, I was intimidated. There were a lot of pieces and hardware. So, I spread them out, picked up each piece, and examined it. IKEA utilizes a pictogram owner's manual. It's just drawings. In fairness, assemblers are frequently encouraged to call IKEA if they get stuck. I didn't call because such experiences can be supremely frustrating. I decided to soldier through.

As I started to assemble the cabinet, I kept re-examining the manual and the individual pieces. I could have used additional information. I even assembled one step incorrectly, and my wife and I had to troubleshoot what I did wrong. I'm happy to report that I proceeded to completion, but it wasn't a straight path from Point A to Point B. I sure could've used timely additional information at crucial junctures of the process.

> **Search for interaction openings.**

Bonding with kids is much more variable-laden than assembling a static piece of furniture. It's a process that must unfold over the entire semester. Many teachers distribute student interest surveys or tease out interesting student passions via icebreaker activities like I promoted in the previous Hack. But such efforts only at the beginning of the semester are not adequate.

THE HACK: COMMIT TO AT LEAST ONE NON-ACADEMIC INTERACTION WITH EACH STUDENT EACH WEEK

Meaningful interactions with students can be exceptionally brief encounters. They can take place in the hallway or the lunchroom. By doing this, you're generating leads. Not leads as in you're trying to sell something but leads to future interactions. Here's how it might work. You notice a student has a cast on their right wrist. You ask what happened and learn that they broke it snow skiing. There's your lead, and you are now set up for your next interaction. You might ask, "Will you return to skiing?" This prompt can lead to an information bonanza. You may hear, "Yes! I love skiing, and I started when I was three." Or, "No! I was talked into going this time, and look what happened." Either way, build off what you learn for your next interaction. Keep repeating this process in a deliberate way.

WHAT YOU CAN DO TOMORROW

- **Keenly observe students.** Search for interaction openings.
- **Engage in interactions outside of class.** This can be in the hallway, the lunchroom, or even in the grocery. When you see students, interact with them, even if the encounter is brief.

- **Follow up on leads.** Use a spreadsheet or calendar to keep track of interactions, if needed. Try to interact and generate a new lead with each student each week.

If you keep generating bonding leads, you'll gain outstanding relationships with students before the semester halfway point, and this will help students to be more engaged in your class.

MANIFEST A VISION

THE PROBLEM: TEACHERS WHO STRUGGLE WITH CLASSROOM MANAGEMENT DON'T KNOW WHERE TO START

WHEN MANY OF my education students describe when they first decided to become teachers, they often depict an idyllic scene from childhood when they created a classroom in their bedroom and transformed their stuffed animals into students. My granddaughter has done this, and it's adorable. But stuffed animals are pretty compliant. Real live kids can be uncooperative and downright obnoxious.

One of my students learned just how difficult classroom management can be when she was placed in a tough situation. A middle school needed a long-term sub to complete the school year. It was April, and the previous teacher had left for personal reasons. This classroom had significant challenges. My student was in her early twenties and had not yet completed her bachelor's degree. She was calm and kind and certainly wasn't an intimidating person. She was unprepared for the difficulties she was about to face from this group of students.

A few weeks into the assignment, she confided in me. She was struggling. She listed her problems:

- The students didn't do their work. A handful of kids set the tone in a negative way. They would frequently disrupt students who were at least nominally compliant.

- Discipline referrals were not a deterrent.

- Other teachers in the building encouraged her to raise her voice and confront students aggressively. This was not in her nature.

- She did find herself "yelling" at the class frequently, and it was totally ineffective.

- She questioned why she ever wanted to become a teacher. This was sad to hear after she had invested so much effort and resources into becoming one. And, she had the potential to become a great teacher.

THE HACK: FORMULATE A VISION OF A BETTER DAY IN THE CLASSROOM

A eureka moment occurred as we brainstormed. I challenged her to describe what a better day would look like. She responded quickly:

- More students would complete their work.

- She would not raise her voice.

- Disruptive students would not bother the ones who were attempting to work.

- She would get along better with the disruptors.

Once we had her objectives, we could game-plan ways to make them materialize. We decided that she would:

1. Post the daily prompt at the beginning of the period.

2. Allow students to wear headphones while they work as long as others can't hear their music.

3. And—and this was the change agent—strive to rein in her reactions.

She had often gotten frustrated and lost her composure, and students don't handle it well when a teacher loses their composure. In many ways, kids can be mirror images of the person in charge.

She started implementing these three objectives the next day, and the situation improved. Within a week, her *Better Day* had been realized, and she was setting more ambitious goals. The biggest benefit was that she looked more relaxed and she was happier. She mentioned that she believed her crucial breakthrough was controlling her emotions. After all, the only thing we can truly control is ourselves. When the semester ended in May, she felt a profound sense of accomplishment and gained a newfound confidence. She even mentioned how she had started developing relationships with some of her past tormentors.

While this is a story about a young teacher finding her sea legs, veteran teachers can also constantly visualize how their class cultures can improve. I do this weekly, even at the college level. Please consider the following ideas.

WHAT YOU CAN DO TOMORROW

- **Make a list.** What student behaviors or classroom procedures are currently unacceptable?
- **Visualize what you want.** What would a better day in your classroom look like?
- **Determine what changes you can make.** Remember how transformative it was for my student to stop losing her composure?

I've taught for almost four decades, and I practice this list frequently. So can you.

107

AMPLIFY EMPATHY

THE PROBLEM: TEACHERS LACK DIRECTION ON HOW TO HELP STUDENTS WITH MENTAL HEALTH CHALLENGES

CONTEMPORARY YOUTH ARE suffering through another pandemic. It's not physical like COVID; it's a mental health crisis. While this observation is purely anecdotal, those who've spent time in twenty-first-century classrooms will likely agree. Few of us are trained mental health professionals. This makes responding appropriately to our students' obstacles particularly challenging. Many students feel totally unhinged in contemporary society, and engagement cannot take place if kids don't feel safe.

This hit home when I began teaching at the college level. I had taught many high school students who suffered from mental health challenges. Generally, a parent and the school mental health support personnel interacted with me, and the youngster remained in class and functioned. Many of these young people ended up thriving. I'm grateful for all the support I received. Some K–12 educators are not so lucky.

It's different at the college level, and I frequently communicate with my students. We interact through text, email, and the Voxer app. It's not unusual the night before class to get a message from an anguished student that reads something like this:

> *I'm so sorry, Mr. Sturtevant. I will not be in class tomorrow. I'm going through a lot right now.*

I once quipped to my wife when a notification beeped on my phone just before bedtime, "I bet I know what this message is about. Some student is informing me they aren't going to make it tomorrow." Unfortunately, I was correct. I regret that remark because it was borne from frustration. My class is simply not as engaging for everyone if students are missing, and absent students miss valuable learning opportunities. My frustration is also generational. I can't imagine sending such a message to one of my professors. My objective is to get over myself and my nostalgia in order to connect with and engage today's young people.

THE HACK: INVESTIGATE, BOND, AND UTILIZE RESOURCES TO BE MORE EMPATHETIC

Picture a struggling student in your class, think of one from your past, or create one from your imagination. How can you proceed with this youngster? The first step is to investigate what resources are available. Speak to their counselor or their case worker. If those resources aren't available, speak to an administrator. See if you can learn some background information about the student. Knowledge will help. After you understand more about what you're contending with, then go to work to forge that bond with the student. Once your relationship starts to evolve, the student may become the greatest resource in terms of helping you to help them overcome learning obstacles.

WHAT YOU CAN DO TOMORROW

- **Empower students to help you help them.** Ask them how you can help when they're struggling. This conversation will be even more fruitful if they're in a good place when you are discussing it. That *good place* may be temporary, so take advantage.

- **Identify your mental health supports.** Find the people in your building who can give you solid advice. Develop a relationship with them. You will need their help in the future.

- **Listen to the experts.** You may feel that kids need to just suck it up and do whatever it is they're avoiding. I confess that I used to experience these feelings. I've come a long way, and I encourage you to follow the advice of mental health professionals and take a more empathetic disposition toward kids who are struggling. Become a safe harbor.

Commit to creating a safe environment for all students. Kids will not engage in your lessons if they don't feel safe. They have a lot more important things to worry about.

108

ASK THE EXPERTS

THE PROBLEM: IT'S HARD TO KNOW WHAT STUDENTS ARE THINKING

S TUDENTS OBSERVE YOU daily. They're experts on you. They probably make comments such as:

- *You got a haircut.*

- *Is that a new shirt?*

- *When did you start wearing glasses?*

- *I saw you at the game last night.*

And yet, in the K–12 world, most teacher evaluations are done by administrators who don't know us nearly as well. When was the last time an administrator made one of those comments to you? The students are only marginally involved in the evaluation process. This should change. If you're brave and you already solicit student feedback—bravo! Now, do it even more.

One mistake that many educators and I have made is feeling smug about our instruction. Such hubris breeds statements like, "My students love when we do X." X can represent a lesson, a tech tool, or a teaching tactic. But how can teachers truly know whether their students love something? I've certainly observed the anecdotal evidence that I was engaging. When my students were enthusiastic about an aspect of class, I felt the warmth of accomplishment. But I didn't inquire more deeply to see if my hunches were accurate.

THE HACK: DEPUTIZE STUDENTS TO BECOME YOUR EVALUATORS

Teaching in higher education has prompted a paradigm shift in me. At the college level, students administer instructor evaluations. I was teaching a wonderful crew of students a few semesters ago, and I was in the zone. The classes flew by. The students were responsive, and their submissions were creative and brilliant. When I received their evaluations via email at the end of the term, I was excited and prepared to break my arm, patting myself on the back for a job well done. The evaluations were great until the last one. It was critical and also fascinating. The student brought up points that I wished they would've voiced during the semester. Such exposure could have created a tremendous teachable moment where all the students and I would evaluate options for my classroom procedures. I acted upon the student's critique the next semester. And guess what? I became a more engaging teacher to all my students. I know this because my evaluations got even better.

This can become a typical post-unit activity. Consider creating anonymous evaluations, such as by using a QR Code linked to an online form. Students can scan the code, answer the questions, and help you become a more engaging educator. Their anonymity should lead to authenticity. It may also lead to some harsh criticism. As hard as it is to read, you can learn from it. In Image 108, you can see the questions my students answered about me.

Sturtevant made the learning target clear.

○ Agree

○ Disagree

○ Not Sure

Sturtevant provided examples of strong and weak work.

○ Agree

○ Disagree

○ Not Sure

Sturtevant provided helpful descriptive feedback.

○ Agree

○ Disagree

○ Not Sure

Image 108: Questions students answered to evaluate their teacher.

WHAT YOU CAN DO TOMORROW

- **Create a teacher evaluation form.** This form should pertain to the unit you're currently navigating with your students.

- **Speculate about what you'll find.** Create a perceived pro and con list. Predict where your students will grade you as strong and where you need to improve.

- **Brace yourself.** Be prepared to read some criticism. This Hack takes guts, but the potential payoff is significant.

Learning what your students think of you as a teacher is a brave step toward becoming the educator you always wanted to be—one who engages and inspires.

109

PASS THE DINNER TABLE TEST

THE PROBLEM: MOST KIDS CAN NO MORE TELL YOU WHAT THEY DID IN SCHOOL THAT DAY THAN THEY CAN FLY

WHEN THE FAMILY gathers at the dinner table or in the car on the way to a practice, parents often inquire about their tender offspring's day at school:

- "How was school today?"

- "What happened at school today?"

- "What did you learn at school today?"

While looking at their phone, the child offspring will often provide meager and unsatisfactory responses:

- "Okay."

- "Nothing."

- "I don't remember."

If you engage students, you have a better chance of inspiring a more thorough, enthusiastic, and positive post-school debriefing. As you read this book, you'll be exposed to many ideas on how to do just that. But to arouse a positive dinner table narrative, you must first effectively set the table in your own classroom.

THE HACK: EMBRACE THE POWER OF THE LEARNING TARGET

When we address learning targets or learning objectives in my Education classes, I promote this idea of passing *The Dinner Table Test*. The test is simple—will your kids be able to answer when prompted about what they learned in school today?

Sadly, learning targets are not utilized enough. When I think back on my teaching tenure, I realize that I could have done a much better job. Every semester, I ask my undergrads the following question: "Think back to every class you've had from kindergarten to college. In the thousands of class periods you've experienced, was a learning target displayed, was it explained, did it make sense, and did you play any role in its creation?" Not one student has answered in the affirmative to every prompt. I'm determined to make up for my past sins of omission and, at the same time, model solid pedagogy to you and my future educators.

Here's the guidance I give my undergrads as a template:

- *Make sure your learning target is visible.* Some teachers write it on the board in big bold script. Others, like me, make it the first slide of the daily presentation. Many, also like me, include it in a classroom syllabus or display it through their school LMS. You can do all of these or a combination. If you want your target to stick, get it out there.

- *Explain your daily learning objective.* After my prompt to students about their history with learning targets, many stated that they often noticed a learning target written on the board when they walked into a class, but the teacher rarely explained it. That's an unwise strategy, but sadly, I'm guilty of this earlier in my career. Such a strategy will often satisfy administrative directives to make your learning targets visible to students, and administrators can easily observe the target. However, the targets won't be impactful unless the teacher explains and promotes them.

- *Write targets in student-friendly language.* This is the only way they'll mean anything to students and perhaps be worthy of mentioning at the dinner table that evening. How would a student write the targets? Compose targets in age-appropriate language. Let's face it: your state's learning standards document doesn't qualify as a page-turner. Most standards are lengthy, dry, clinical, and populated with education jargon. Take a long standard and chunk it into smaller, manageable directives. Make it empowering as in the famous *I can* statement: *I can create a model that …*

- *And finally, guide kids to collaborate to transform a state standard into targets that make sense to them.* If you're interested in students taking ownership of their learning, this is a powerful tactic.

WHAT YOU CAN DO TOMORROW

- **Display your target.** Don't worry about overkill. Paste it on your syllabus and in your LMS. Write it on the board. Insert it into a slide presentation.

- **Explain your target.** Don't just post it; talk about it. Many kids don't bother reading words just because you wrote them on the board.

- **Compose a relevant target.** Keep it short. Make it empowering. Write it with words that your students will understand.

- **Challenge your students to create a target.** This is a powerful tactic that inspires ownership.

Follow these steps, and you'll have a better chance of students understanding and talking about what they are learning in your class when they are at the dinner table.

CLEAR THE HIGHER-LEVEL-THINKING BAR

THE PROBLEM: LOWER-LEVEL THINKING PROMPTS DON'T INSPIRE ENGAGEMENT, AND WE ISSUE TOO MANY OF THEM

A COUPLE OF WEEKS into a new semester, I ask my students, "How many of you could do well on last semester's final exams if you had to take them again today?" A few will respond that they could duplicate their previous results. However, when I prompt students to recall a past learning experience that was highly engaging, many will point to a capstone project, a model they built, a demonstration they designed, or a performance they created. They can tell me the details of these experiences and describe what they learned. Many of their examples are not from a previous semester but from years ago. Some students recall learning experiences from elementary school!

This story illustrates a problem in contemporary education. Much of what we ask kids to do is of the lower-level-thinking, short-term-memory variety. This is particularly true of summative assessments. My students' last semester final exams apparently didn't have much shelf life.

Recall your Education classes in college. Your classes probably discussed Benjamin Bloom's taxonomy. Although Bloom's template has been around for decades and gone through revisions, the classic rendition still has tremendous relevance in today's classrooms. His pyramidal taxonomy is a user-friendly lesson-design template. The verbs you use indicate the appropriate level of thinking. Here are examples:

- I can remember — Level 1

- I can apply — Level 3

- I can evaluate — Level 5

- I can create — Level 6

The higher the level, the higher the thinking. The higher the thinking, the higher the engagement. But rest assured, we still need lower-level thinking. To lay the foundation for higher-level thinking, I often conduct a brief, direct instruction session, or I have students master a resource.

I want students to understand what cooperative learning is before we dive into the heart of the lesson, which involves evaluating and creating.

THE HACK: INTRODUCE YOUR STUDENTS TO BENJAMIN BLOOM

While most educators are familiar with Bloom and his template, few students are aware. Why are we keeping this template a secret? My guess is that we don't think it will have any relevance to kids.

I introduce Bloom's template in the following fashion. First, I display the template and describe the levels (lower-level thinking with direct instruction). Next, I challenge them to apply the template by comparing it to the learning process that they went through when they developed a passion for a hobby (mid-level thinking where students work independently or collaboratively). And finally, I prompt them to create a plan to teach this hobby to someone else (the highest realm of Bloom's taxonomy where students create something).

The previous Hack promoted the student creation of learning targets, and this Hack builds off that skill. You can offer students a learning target you created, which calls for lower-level thinking, and ask them to transform it to satisfy higher levels of Bloom's taxonomy. Or, you could have students refine the target they created into directives that will satisfy different levels of the pyramid.

WHAT YOU CAN DO TOMORROW

- **Prompt students about previous engaging learning experiences.** You'll be greeted with lots of projects and performances. Make certain to follow up. Ask them what was so engaging about these experiences.
- **Challenge students to apply Bloom's taxonomy to a hobby.** This is a great tactic to make an abstract concept more relevant.
- **Prompt students to transform learning targets.** You can take this process all the way from a state standard to providing lower-level thinking targets and asking them to transform them.

When students are actively involved in lesson planning, it is a wonderful buy-in pathway. It is also an excellent example of engaging higher-level thinking.

111

COLLABORATE ON A VIRTUAL LANDING PAD

THE PROBLEM: STUDENTS NEED A SIMPLIFIED AND POWERFUL WAY TO SUBMIT WORK

GOOGLE IS PREVALENT in K–12, but in many higher education venues, like where I'm teaching now, Microsoft rules. My administration tolerates my Google preference because I'm teaching future K–12 educators, and Google will probably be the tool they utilize. You can use basic Google tools for this Hack, but you can also use Carrd, Mailchimp, or HubSpot.

Collaboration is foundational, and it enhances engagement. That goes for collaboration between students and teachers and peer-to-peer. It is an essential learning step because it fuels revision.

The learning management system at my university is Blackboard. It's an impressive system stocked with features and capabilities, including collaborative ones. Your district's LMS probably does too. Learn to use all of the collaboration features you can, but understand that many learning management systems have significant security safeguards that can make collaboration more cumbersome.

THE HACK: MORPH A BASIC DOCUMENT INTO A COLLABORATIVE LANDING PAD

You can use a humble online document to facilitate collaboration. Merely copy your class roster and paste it onto a document, then label it *The Landing Pad*. Adjust the share settings on this document to *Can Edit*, which allows students to submit their work. Then, provide students with a link to the Landing Pad Doc at the bottom of a prompt. (If needed, instruct students on how to insert a URL into any document.) Highlight the words *Landing Pad* and then insert the URL for the Landing Pad Doc so the words become blue and underlined. Students will have no problem navigating to the Landing Pad Doc, where they'll find their names nestled in with their classmates. This is where they'll submit links to their work. Image 111 shows a screenshot of four students in a fictitious class of Greek deities. As you can see by the underlined hyperlinks, the goddesses have turned in their work while the gods are procrastinating. At the top of the document, I provide links to a strong example and a weak example to help guide my students.

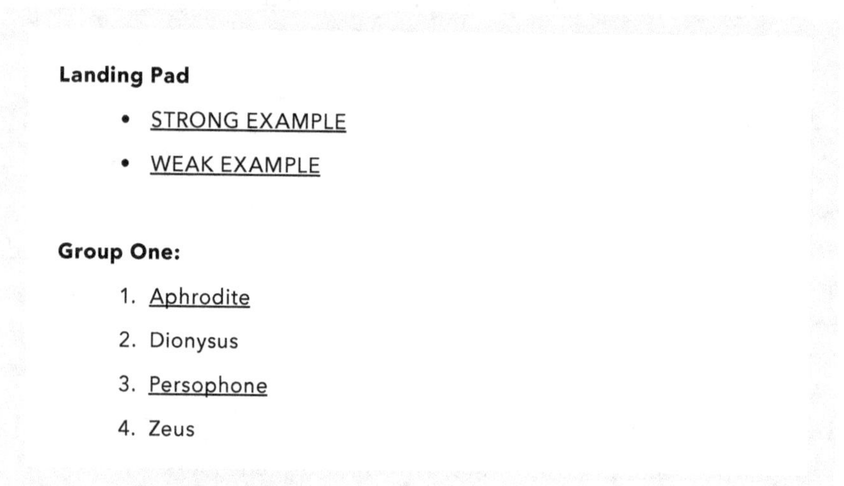

Landing Pad

- <u>STRONG EXAMPLE</u>
- <u>WEAK EXAMPLE</u>

Group One:

1. <u>Aphrodite</u>
2. Dionysus
3. <u>Persophone</u>
4. Zeus

Image 111: A virtual Landing Pad page with hyperlinks.

You'll find many advantages to using a landing pad document, including:

Accountability: At any point, a teacher can see who has submitted work and who has not. In the Image 111 example, the teacher may want to reach out to Dionysus and Zeus.

Collaboration: You can encourage students to submit rough drafts early. Then you can comment by inserting narratives on their submission, providing virtual feedback, or collaborating in person. Students can then revise their submissions, and you can see what they've done and offer even more feedback, which can inspire additional revision. You can even instruct your students to review their classmates' submissions. Peer feedback can carry more weight than adult feedback.

Guidance: Examples of past student work are a powerful learning beacon. You can show kids what to do and what not to do. You can even give them student examples and let them evaluate—they can determine which is the strong and weak example and figure out why.

WHAT YOU CAN DO TOMORROW

- **Copy your roster and paste it on a document Landing Pad.** Arrange students into small groups to facilitate collaboration.

- **Adjust the share settings.** Make sure your Landing Pad's settings are set to *Can Edit* so students can insert their URLs, and your students have adjusted their submission settings to *Can View* so you and their classmates can see what they've done.

- **Consider ways to utilize the Landing Pad for collaboration.** Make a list of how you'll use *The Landing Pad* to collaborate with individual students and how you'll foster peer-to-peer collaboration.

- **Include examples of previous student submissions.** This is an important inclusion and can help guide students.

A basic document Landing Pad can help you achieve all these ends in a way that is straightforward, efficient, and organized.

112

GIVE THE GIFT OF GIFS

THE PROBLEM: GIFS ARE NOT TAKEN SERIOUSLY BY EDUCATORS

RECENTLY DEMONSTRATED PROGRESS monitoring to my education students in an engaging way. I told them I had been one of the best sprinters on my high school track team. Now I'm in my sixties, and for some odd reason, I decided I wanted to start sprinting again. Many of my friends and family members thought it was a ridiculous objective. My sprinting quest turned into a marvelous way to demonstrate a slow evolution to a goal—progress monitoring.

This was an eighteen-month quest. Amazingly, it felt so good to run down our high school's turf football field as fast as I could. I felt forty years younger, and then, unfortunately, reality set in. I timed myself. *Wow.* I was a lot slower than I used to be. The numbers were confirmed when I videoed myself with my phone. It was shocking to see but also humorous. I showed the video to my students. They also thought it was hilarious; however, they were more complimentary than I anticipated. I decided to keep sprinting. And this, dear reader, is where my story takes a fantastic turn. I decided to use GIFs to demonstrate the complex idea of progress monitoring for a sprinter.

THE HACK: PROMPT STUDENTS TO EMPLOY GIFS TO DEMONSTRATE A COMPLEX IDEA

I wanted to demonstrate progress monitoring in a novel but understandable way. Most students have life goals, so I was confident they could relate to my objective of sprinting seven yards in one second. When I started sprinting again, I could only cover six yards in one second. I decided to demonstrate progress monitoring, limiting myself to a one-page Google Doc, three GIFs, and limited text. The first three-second GIF was from the summer of 2021, and I covered six yards per second. The second GIF was from the winter of 2022, and I covered 6.5 yards per second. And the final GIF was from the summer of 2022. I hit my goal of seven yards per second six months early! So, just as you would do with your students, I had to adjust my objective. Image 112 shows a screenshot of what I presented to my students—although the still image is weak sauce compared to the GIF-infused original, where I'm sprinting back and forth in front of my students' eyes.

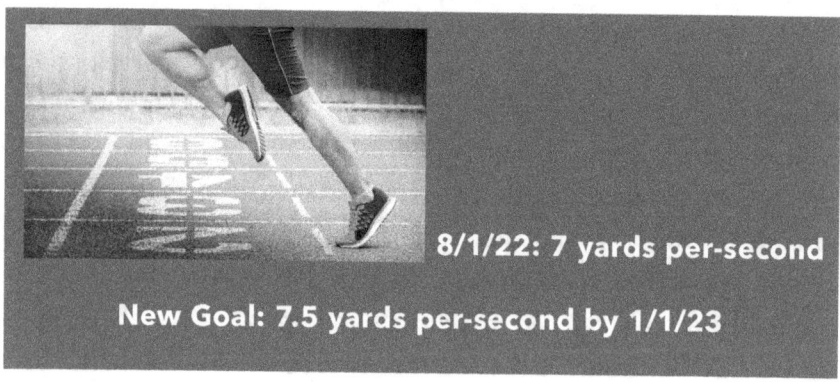

8/1/22: 7 yards per-second

New Goal: 7.5 yards per-second by 1/1/23

Image 112: A still image from a GIF I showed my students as an example of progress monitoring.

I love how I was able to demonstrate this story to my students with just thirty-six words and three GIFs. Look for ways you can challenge your students to tell a story about a complex idea in a similar fashion.

Creating a GIF is remarkably easy. Try the GIFit! Chrome extension. Once you add it to your Chrome account, a GIFit! icon appears on every YouTube video that you watch. Adjust the recording time to three seconds. That's a good length for a GIF. You download the GIF just like any other image and then insert it into a document. Your students can also utilize Giphy, the popular GIF platform. Students can make GIFs starring themselves or use any YouTube video. (You may want to research your district's policy, but generally, creating GIFs from copyrighted work is considered fair use, especially when it is for nonprofit or educational purposes.) Remind students that GIFs don't have sound. Limit your students to a one-page document with less than fifty words of text and no more than three GIFs. They'll have fun with this higher-level-thinking creation challenge.

WHAT YOU CAN DO TOMORROW

- **Create a GIF.** Explore the GIF-creating platforms GIFit! and Giphy, plus any other options you wish. The key is to create a file that is easy to download and insert into a document.

- **Give a prompt.** Think about a complex concept or an evolution that students can demonstrate. Utilizing GIFs can be challenging for some kids. Be prepared to help them brainstorm.

- **Formulate a display format.** Once students create their one-page online document populated with three GIFs, have them share it with classmates. A great submission will inspire class discussion, which means engagement.

If a picture is worth a thousand words, imagine the story a three-second video can tell.

CHAMPION SELF-ASSESSMENT

THE PROBLEM: STUDENTS ARE NOT ENGAGED IN THE IMPORTANT PROCESS OF PROGRESS MONITORING

ADULTS DO TOO much for kids. I'm certainly guilty of this; I did too much as a parent, and I've done too much as a teacher. My intention has always been noble, but I fear that I instead served as an enabler at times.

Interestingly, as I've aged, I've become better at recognizing when I'm doing too much for students. I still work hard for them, but I've come to recognize the engagement power of allowing them to do more of what they are capable of doing. A rich student empowerment opportunity exists in the important realm of progress monitoring.

> *Guide the students to generate their own objectives.*

In my Assessment class, we delve deeply into progress monitoring. It's the way teachers can prove to parents, administrators, and, most importantly, students that learning is taking place within their classrooms. At times, students may feel like lab rats in the process. Progress monitoring terminology, like baselines and probes, doesn't help kids feel less rodent-like. Transforming students into active self-monitors is a way to not only engage them in this important process but to increase the chances they'll become invested in their growth—feeling more like participants and less like subjects.

THE HACK: GUIDE STUDENTS TO CREATE A PROGRESS MONITORING GRAPH USING A SPREADSHEET

You can take two approaches with this Hack. The first is to ask students to self-monitor an academic objective that you create, like how many words they can read in one minute. The second is to guide the students to generate their own objectives. The goals students generate on their own can be fascinating. I've seen students choose goals such as:

- How many periods can I go without looking at social media?

- How many books can I read in one semester?

- How many days can I go without a discipline referral?

Sometimes, students come up with a goal that is darned near impossible to measure, or they come up empty and can't think of a goal. In either case, be prepared to help them or give them one.

Image 113.1 shows the steps to create a progress monitoring graph in an online spreadsheet. I'll use my ridiculous old man sprinting example from the previous Hack. I've used this example successfully in my Assessment class.

Step 1: In Column A, list the starting date and ending date, and in between, list the dates for periodic probes.

Step 2: In Column C, put the beginning point at the top and then the objective at the bottom. You want to create a straight goal line on your graph. To do this, you must set intermediate goals that coincide with the periodic probe dates. These intermediate goals must be spaced uniformly to create a straight line. In my example, my objective was to improve by one-third of a yard on each probe date.

Step 3: In Column B, record the probe results. You will fill in this column from top to bottom as the progress monitoring phase unfolds.

Step 4: To create your graph, highlight all the data on the Google Sheet and then select *Insert* and then *Chart*. Select *Line Graph* when prompted.

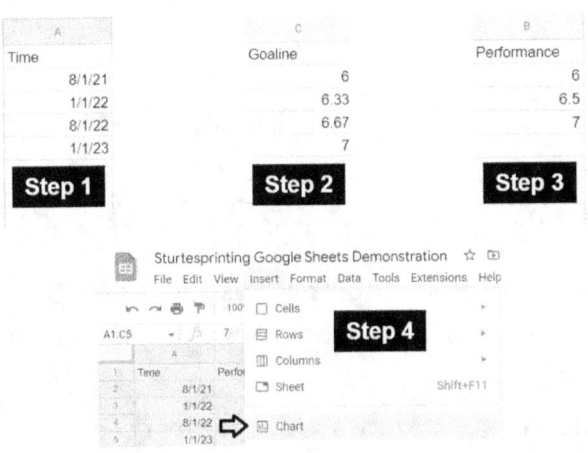

Image 113.1: Sturtevant's sprinting spreadsheet.

After you insert the results from each probe, the graph will change to reflect the new status quo. Students can see exactly how they're doing based on their objectives. You can collaborate with them to either brainstorm interventions, improve performance, or adjust the goal line because it was too modest. That's what this old man needs to do with my sprinting goals (see Image 113.2). I underestimated myself!

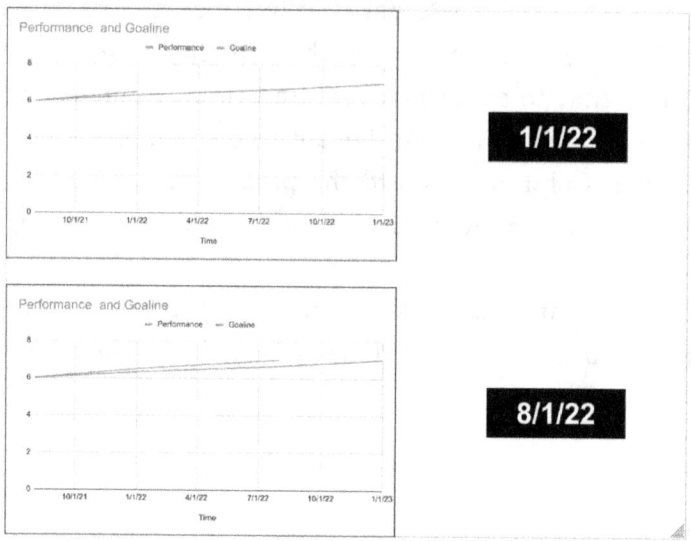

Image 113.2: This graph inspired me toward a more ambitious goal.

WHAT YOU CAN DO TOMORROW

- **Create a graph using spreadsheets.** Keep track of what data goes in what column. Complete Column C before Column B.

- **Decide what students will monitor.** This can be a goal you create or one they create.

- **Prompt students to create a graph.** After you've mastered how to create the graph using a spreadsheet app, develop a plan for how you will walk them through the steps.

Progress monitoring will have so much more impact if the students are intimately involved in the process. Using spreadsheets and graphs can be fun, motivating, and even a source of pride.

FIRE UP THE RANDOM NAME GENERATOR

THE PROBLEM: MANY STUDENTS WON'T VOLUNTEER TO PARTICIPATE IN CLASS

A FEW YEARS AGO when I was teaching high school, I had an interesting World Civilization class. Three kids in the class were passionate historians. When I tossed out a prompt, they chomped at the bit in unbridled enthusiasm. They put up their hands and demanded to be called on. The remaining twenty students would sit silently—either too intimidated or too embarrassed to offer an observation in the shadows of these future doctoral candidates.

This was not satisfactory. My class was ultra-engaging for just a sliver of my students. Most of my kids were relegated to semi-engaged observers. I certainly didn't want to dampen the enthusiasm of my go-getters, but I wanted to ignite the participation of my wallflowers.

I tried to become more intentional about whom I called on: different students, those who didn't have their hands up, or students who didn't appear exceptionally engaged. While such an effort was noble, it didn't seem effective. When I was in the throes of teaching a lesson, I didn't want to be distracted by having to inventory whom I had and hadn't called upon. Implicit bias was a likely factor as well. Calling on students is a selection process, and certain unrecognized variables influenced my choices. I wanted to find a selection process that was random and required little effort. (You can find a related Hack in the original *Hacking Engagement* book.)

THE HACK: CREATE A RANDOM NAME GENERATOR WITH A SPREADSHEET

A basic spreadsheet became my answer to my student-selection problem. You can paste in your class roster, and with two clicks of the mouse, it formulates the list in a random order.

Image 114 illustrates the steps to use the *Random Name Generator*. And since I referenced my past history class, I created a short class roster comprised of Greek deities. (As you can imagine, this collection of students could produce a lot of drama!) Once you've copied and pasted your roster into a spreadsheet, randomize the order by simply selecting the *Data* tab and then the *Randomize Range* option. The student whose name appears at the top of the list is the one you call upon next: "Dionysus, what's your reaction to …?"

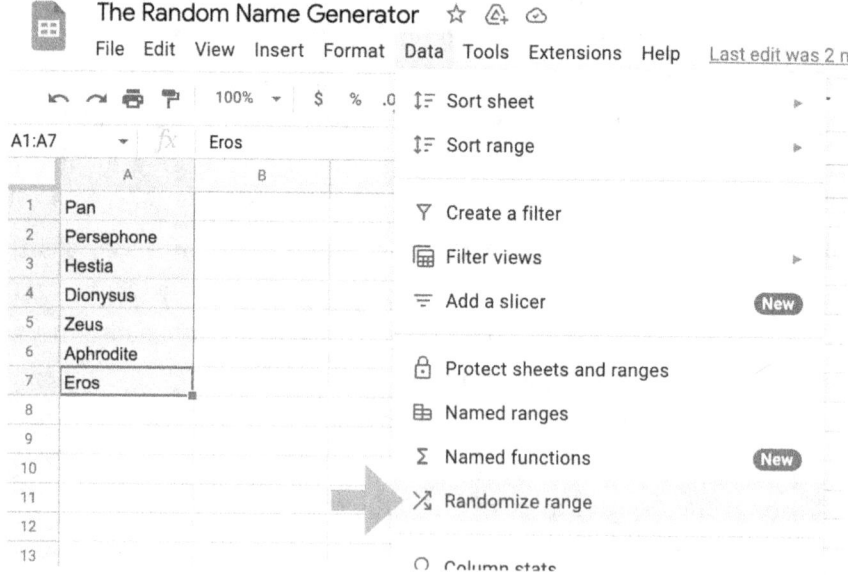

Image 114: The *Random Name Generator* steps.

You may be concerned about putting introverted students on the spot when their names materialize at the top of the generator. Consider offering a *No-Fault Wave Off*. Any student who is uncomfortable answering can wave you off with no questions asked. You can also activate the generator before you ask the question. Then, when you see the student's name, you can go to your bank of questions and choose the one you think will fit that student best. Introverted student management is an important variable.

When you project this spreadsheet onto your classroom screen and then transform it via the randomizer, it creates anticipation in students, like watching a roulette wheel spin in Monte Carlo. The randomization process, in itself, becomes highly engaging.

WHAT YOU CAN DO TOMORROW

- **Copy and paste your class roster into the spreadsheet.** This takes mere seconds. If your students are listed in alphabetical order by last name, but their first names appear first, the spreadsheet can easily sort them alphabetically by their first names.

- **Apply the randomization steps.** Practice a few times before you try it with students. Project the spreadsheet on the screen so students can watch whose name appears at the top after every randomizer click. My policy is that if a student's name appears at the top more than once in a period, I sort the roster again.

- **Deputize a kid to be the Randomizer Du Jour.** This is a fun detour. You can share the online spreadsheet with a student, adjust the share settings, and let them become the randomizer. They'll enjoy calling out the next classmate's name.

- **Create prompts for your unveiling.** Designate about four meaty prompts for your first voyage. Once you get comfortable with this technique, you can use it more.

The *Random Name Generator* creates a low-stakes opportunity for all kids to participate. Students will also get a kick out of watching the generator in action.

FIND THE FLOW

THE PROBLEM: SOME TOPICS IN YOUR CURRICULUM ARE TEDIOUS

'M CURRENTLY TEACHING two boring-sounding undergraduate classes. Curriculum and Design is taught to third-year students who also must take my Assessment course. There's no option at my university other than taking these classes from little ole me. The challenge of taking dry material and making it engaging motivates me. I've spent many enjoyable hours in the waning summer months planning, scheming, creating, experimenting, and anticipating. I'm a great choice for teaching Curriculum and Design because I truly love designing lessons. (I know, it's not an interest that anyone should put on a dating site profile.) The challenge for me is to inspire my students to learn to love lesson planning as well. Perhaps you can learn to enjoy it even more too.

When I'm hiking with my wife, working out, writing, woodworking, or doing lesson planning, I often find myself in a flow state. In other words, I'm highly engaged and enjoying the creation process. When in such a state, I've migrated out of any awareness of the space-time continuum. When I teach using the Hacks in this book, most of them have had similar flow-inducing effects on my students.

That's why I included them in this collection. Often, students glance up at the clock near the end of the period and are shocked that time has evaporated. That, dear friend, is engagement gold.

THE HACK: CHALLENGE STUDENTS TO HELP CREATE THE FLOW STATE

Devote effort at first to helping your students understand the concept of flow. Employ a random sorter to your class roster, as I promoted in the previous Hack. After your kids are randomized, break them into small groups. Ask them to take turns talking about what they love to do. Encourage them to choose an activity they enjoy so much that they lose track of time. Ask them to briefly share why they love this activity, and give groups about five minutes for this phase. Once the time expires, challenge each group to select a member to represent them. This can be a student who provided an interesting share or one who shared in a highly engaging way.

Moderate doses of negative thinking have served me well.

These selected individuals will then give their elevator pitches to the entire class. They'll describe their understanding of flow and how their examples demonstrate this sought-after state.

Next, direct students to take your learning target and formulate ways they could create a flow state to master the directive. Send them back to their groups and challenge them to come up with at least one idea to help create the flow state. This is a tall task for most kids. You're asking them to become enthusiastic about something they don't want to be enthusiastic about. But, guess what? They generally come up with neat ideas. Only give groups five minutes to create their plans. When time is up, prompt every group to select a new spokesperson, and direct them to provide at least one idea to the class. Great suggestions could include diverse ways for students to demonstrate learning or a suggestion for a creative learning environment.

WHAT YOU CAN DO TOMORROW

- **Choose a boring lesson.** If you dread teaching a lesson or unit, I'll bet your students feel your pain.
- **Provide examples.** Provide personal examples of activities that put you in a flow state.
- **Group students randomly.** Reference the *Random Name Generator* from Hack 114.
- **Prompt them to brainstorm.** Encourage students to evaluate personal examples of being in a flow state and speculate on ways they can help you make a boring lesson engaging.

Your creative students may come up with amazing ideas that will transform your lesson and engage students who must navigate this once-dull lesson for the rest of your career.

DISPLAY SOME BLING

PROBLEM: TEACHERS RARELY CONSIDER VISUAL APPEAL WHEN DESIGNING INSTRUCTIONAL MATERIAL

THIS BOOK IS about engaging students. Students are humans, and you're a human, too, so your engagement is vital as well. When a teacher is highly engaged in the art of inspiring learning, their students reap the benefits.

I promote the concept of flow—the idea that you're in this creative, desirable, euphoric state where space and time fade into the background. When I discuss flow with others, most conversers will describe a flow scenario involving a cherished hobby. When I discuss flow with fellow teachers, they'll typically respond in a similar fashion. I have yet to meet a teacher who has designated "lesson planning" as their flow-state inducer.

Lesson planning has this effect on me. You may find that hard to believe, but it's true. My paradigm shifted when I started working with HyperDocs. (See Hack 52 in the book *Hacking Engagement Again*.) I've utilized them every day in the classroom ever since. HyperDocs are merely attractive document templates that you can manipulate to fit your purposes. Please search HyperDocs and explore the templates.

Before HyperDocs made a dramatic appearance in my teaching life, I didn't give too much thought to how my lessons appeared.

Once I started toying with creating beautiful lessons and prompts, planning became more engaging. While I use HyperDocs, I populate the documents with provocative and beautiful images, GIFs I find and GIFs I create, colorful QR codes, and a bevy of hyperlinked phrases.

THE HACK: CREATE BEAUTIFUL INSTRUCTIONAL MATERIAL

I was asked to teach Education Technology a couple of semesters ago, and I enthusiastically agreed. The department head shared the syllabus, which was like other college syllabi—fifteen white pages of blah, blah, blah. Most students just want to know what's due and when, and how they'll be assessed. There are certainly exceptions, but most don't read the entire syllabus.

I reviewed the old syllabus and thought, *I'm being asked to teach an Education Technology class. I certainly can produce a syllabus that looks better than this.* In the months leading up to the semester, I read the text, formulated the capstone project, and constructed weekly HyperDocs prompts to support the capstone.

Somewhere along this journey of creation, I became obsessed with creating a cool-looking, one-stop-shop, one-page PDF syllabus. I found a platform called Lucidchart, which was perfect for my objective. Lucidchart allows you to manipulate shapes, insert hyperlinks, and download what you've created as a PDF. I decided on a pyramidal-shaped syllabus because it reinforces my commitment to Bloom's taxonomy and it creates the perfect platform for the capstone project. Each block of the pyramid contains a link to the weekly HyperDoc and a description of the weekly higher-level-thinking prompt. The two circles on each side of the pyramid contain contact information and links to the traditional long syllabus.

I was euphoric when a student commented about how much they loved my syllabus. Wouldn't it be cool to hear your students praise something that you created and find value in it? See an example of my syllabus in Image 116.

517 Syllabus and Course Structure

James Sturtevant
jsturtev@muskingum.edu
Voxer
Contact information

WEEK 10:
11/15 - 12/3
Please submit your
Capstone Project

Expanded Syllabus
Textbook
Weekly Teams Chat
Resources

WEEK 8:
11/1 - 11/8
We'll master concepts from Chapter 7 and then create a StoryMap. Please master the Week 8 HyperDoc.

WEEK 9:
11/8 - 11/15
We'll create a professional development session based on a topic from this semester. Please master the Week 9 HyperDoc.

WEEK 5:
10/11 - 10/18
We'll master concepts from the second portion of Chapter 4 and then create a Project Based Learning prompt that is based on a state learning standard. Please master the Week 5 HyperDoc.

WEEK 6:
10/18 - 10/25
We'll master concepts from Chapter 5 and then create a video on information Literacy. Please master the Week 6 HyperDoc.

WEEK 7:
10/25 - 11/1
We'll master concepts from Chapter 6 and then create a whiteboard activity. Please master the Week 7 HyperDoc.

WEEK 1:
9/13 - 9/20
We'll master concepts from Chapter 1 and then create a Quizlet Live session. Please master the Week 1 HyperDoc.

WEEK 2:
9/20 - 9/27
We'll master concepts from Chapter 2 and then create a student-friendly learning target and a 21st Century Skills Google Drawing. Please master the Week 2 HyperDoc.

WEEK 3:
9/27 - 10/4
We'll master concepts from Chapter 3 and then create a HyperDoc. Please master the Week 3 HyperDoc.

WEEK 4:
10/4 - 10/11
We'll master concepts from the first portion of Chapter 4 and then create a Project Based Learning StoryBoardThat. Please master the Week 4 HyperDoc.

Image 116: An example of my syllabus and course structure design.

WHAT YOU CAN DO TOMORROW

- **Designate a lesson, a prompt, or an entire syllabus for a remodel.** Your school's learning management system may also have design tools that you can utilize.

- **Explore HyperDocs.** This is still one of my absolute favorite lesson-design sites.

- **Explore Lucidchart.** I utilized this site for my one-page syllabus. You can also create a comprehensive document for your class. If you issue a capstone project, consider my pyramidal design.

- **Embed hyperlinks.** I like the one-stop-shop nature of my syllabus. When you include hyperlinks, you can send your students to exotic places from a beautifully designed and centrally located document.

Transform the educational material you design by focusing on visual appeal. The next time you're creating a lesson, you might find yourself in a flow state as you generate content that engages your students.

STAGE A HAIKU SLAM

THE PROBLEM: ARTISTIC EXPRESSION IS RARELY PRESENT IN CORE SUBJECTS

LESSONS FEATURING EAST Asian art were my favorite back when I taught World Civilization to high school students. Typically, the focus of Western art is on the individual, and the focus of East Asian art is on harmony—something larger than the individual, such as nature or the universal flow, as promoted in Daoism. A wonderful manifestation of subtle yet powerful Asian art is the humble Japanese haiku. A haiku is a three-line poem. The first line contains five syllables, the second line contains seven, and the third line contains five. These diminutive, melodious poems are not, however, lacking in impact. They tend to inspire wonder.

Twitter and Instagram are also populated with short messages. But social media posts, unfortunately, are often saturated with self-promotion or designed to agitate opponents. Social media also produces wonder—as in, *I wonder why I feel so inadequate after looking at these posts?* Creating a haiku will be healthier for your kids.

Integrating haiku into lessons is a great strategy because students thrive when challenged to express themselves artistically. We certainly don't do this enough in core subjects.

THE HACK: PROMPT STUDENTS TO DEMONSTRATE A COMPLEX CONCEPT WITH A HAIKU

Image 117 shows a haiku I created to describe this book. It's not easy to be impactful in just three lines and to limit each line to the correct number of syllables. I paired my haiku with an image that I took while hiking with my wife in Southern Tennessee. I love how the river matches the sky, and the reflective water embodies the concept of flow. I posted this haiku on Padlet, but any public display venue will work for your class. Make certain to count the syllables in each line.

**Fuel deep learning with
the sweet flow of engagement.
Empower students.**

Image 117: A haiku example along with a photo of Snoopers Rock in Tennessee.

Create student groups of three. These groups can be chosen by design or random. Once sorted, students collaborate collectively, or they divide and conquer. If they allocate roles, offer these guidelines:

1. One student can work out what ideas they need to include.

2. One can work on syllable management.

3. One can find the perfect image. They might locate appropriate images online on a platform like Unsplash, or they can pull one from their phones.

They can also choose how they will present their haiku. Perhaps each student will be responsible for presenting one line.

The Padlet looks cool once all of the student groups post their haiku. It's fun to hear the kids present their submissions. (This is similar to a Haiku Slam event.) It became clear to me the first time I issued this prompt that students must truly understand a concept in order to create an effective haiku about it.

WHAT YOU CAN DO TOMORROW

- **Select a complex concept.** Choose one from your curriculum that students find challenging to understand and explain.

- **Sort students into groups of three.** You can divide your roster by three. For example, if you have twenty-four students, form eight groups of three. Or, you can have the class nominate the eight most creative students. These students become the artistic directors. The remaining sixteen students are randomly assigned to a creative director. Or, you can sort your roster randomly with the *Random Name Generator* mentioned in Hack 114. It's fine if you end up with a couple of groups of two or four if the roster is not perfectly divisible.

- **Prompt students to collaborate on an approach.** They can divide up into specific roles or collaborate on all aspects of their haiku creation.

- **Issue the haiku prompt.** Students will benefit from reading and hearing examples of traditional haiku. But this is one prompt where you may want to avoid displaying examples of past student work. You don't want your students' freshly percolating ideas to be influenced by other student work.

- **Determine the presentation mode.** Decide whether your class will do best with a Padlet, a Google Slide presentation, or another public display medium. Encourage students to snap their fingers enthusiastically instead of clapping at the conclusion of each haiku presentation. Make your classroom like a coffee house in Soho in 1958.

When students are challenged to collaboratively explain a complex subject artistically, it facilitates understanding and stokes higher-level thinking. Just be prepared. If your kids like their haiku creation, they'll most likely post it on Instagram.

INSPIRE AMBITIOUS GOALS

THE PROBLEM: STUDENTS DON'T KNOW MUCH ABOUT THEIR TEACHERS

MY BROTHER-IN-LAW'S BROTHER-IN-LAW (no, I am not describing myself) is Anthony Morales from Beaumont, Texas. He's in his late sixties, he's a former Marine, and he loves to challenge himself physically. He's an age-defying beast, and I love interacting with him when he visits Ohio. I once told him that I'd love to join him on one of his fitness quests. The next day, he returned to Texas, and I largely forgot about the conversation. Just two weeks after his visit, however, Tony called me with an offer. I learned that you must be careful what you ask for.

He explained that he and a group of guys were going to hike the Grand Canyon. I'd read about these hikes. If you go rim to rim, you're going to walk twenty-four miles with five thousand feet of elevation change. That's a formidable hike, but I was confident I could do it. However, I misunderstood what Tony was proposing. He wanted me to hike rim to rim to rim—going down and up twice. That equates to forty-eight miles with eleven thousand feet of elevation change. And Tony and his Band of Brothers were planning to do it nonstop.

I was sixty years old when Tony proposed this hike. The hike would be challenging for someone in their prime. It was an intimidating proposition, and after two days of vacillating, I committed. My Hernan Cortes *Burn the Ships* moment came when I bought my plane tickets.

THE HACK: SHARE A GOAL WITH YOUR STUDENTS

I shared my objective with my students, and they were on board immediately. Fueled by their enthusiasm, I detailed my training plans. I talked about gear, provisions, and sleeping arrangements. As the weeks progressed and the hike loomed, I provided detailed progress monitoring. I charted my hiking distances, took pictures of my practice hikes, and shared them with students outside of class time via the Voxer app. When I confessed my concerns, I was amazed at the support I received, such as "We know you can do it, Mr. Sturtevant!" Students kept asking a lot of questions. They were hooked.

In October of 2021, I walked from the South Rim to the North Rim and then back to the South Rim. I covered forty-eight miles, I climbed eleven thousand feet, and it took me twenty-nine hours. (See Image 118.) I was elated, and so were my students. They supported me every step of the way—literally. In the process, we learned a lot about one another.

Now it's your turn. Share an ambitious goal with your students, and then keep sharing as you detail your completion journey. You'll become more familiar and approachable to your students. They just might start sharing some of their goals with you. Wouldn't that be awesome?

WHAT YOU CAN DO TOMORROW

- **Formulate a goal.** Make this goal something you're passionate about enough to see it through. That doesn't mean you have to achieve it. In some ways, it might help kids to see their teacher strive, fall short, and then reformulate. It's okay to show them that you're mortal.

- **Share your objective with students.** Consider engaging ways that you can share your goal. Display beautiful images and have students guess the reason. Once kids start guessing, signal to them that they're getting warmer or colder. This investigation will be engaging to them as well.

- **Monitor progress.** Share evidence of your preparation or progress, and describe your approach to attaining your goal. You can even share graphs like in traditional progress monitoring. Detail successes and setbacks. Tell an engaging story.

If you share a personal goal with your kids, they'll help you achieve it. In the process, you'll be a wonderful inspirational example. Wow, were my students proud of me, and I learned more about them in the process! This scenario naturally builds student engagement inside and outside of school.

Image 118: Sturtevant at the top of the Grand Canyon South Rim.

119

CONDUCT A NEGATIVE THOUGHT EXPERIMENT

THE PROBLEM: EDUCATORS CAN APPEAR POLLYANNAISH

I N THE PREVIOUS Hack, I recounted how I achieved the audacious goal of completing the rim-to-rim-to-rim hike in the Grand Canyon. I love telling that story, but there have also been many times when I've created an ambitious goal, I didn't achieve it, and then I lost interest in my objective. A few years back, I became intoxicated by performing the Olympic snatch with my body weight. It's a highly technical lift with injury potential. I pursued this objective unsuccessfully for a while, and then I gave up. Now, I rarely perform this exercise.

Sometimes, we educators overdo it with positive thinking. Some students might view our frequent growth mindset sermons as frivolous or, worse, a bit phony. Now make no mistake: it's great to frequently promote optimistic solutions, but maybe we need more balance.

Sarah Elizabeth Adler wrote a fascinating article in *The Atlantic* called "The Power of Negative Thinking." She argues that individuals who embrace negative thinking are more generous and successful in accomplishing their goals. Interesting. I used to teach Economics, and Personal Finance was my favorite unit. Thinking back, I realize this unit promoted a balanced approach to wealth creation. Students were encouraged to systematically invest (play offense) and prepare for hardship by creating a rainy-day reserve and adding insurance protection (play defense). We also focused on the pitfalls of over-spending with credit cards. This unit included a lot of negative thinking.

A few years ago, I was greeted in the grocery by a smiling older couple. I recognized them once they identified their son, whom I'd had as a student. By this point, their son was in his late thirties. They mentioned that he frequently cited that Economics unit we'd navigated as instrumental to his financial success. This experience came back to me when I read the article in *The Atlantic*. We engaged in negative thinking in that unit. Our wealth-creation goals were tempered by strategizing for potential pitfalls.

THE HACK: CHALLENGE STUDENTS TO SPECULATE ABOUT OBSTACLES

This Hack is like threading a needle. Many students, unfortunately, are negative-thinking all-stars. You hate to pour gasoline on their crabby fires. You also hate to pour cold water on smoldering, audacious dreams. Think of telling the young Michael Jordan after he was cut from his high school basketball team, "Why don't you think of another goal besides playing in the NBA?" But there aren't many Michael Jordans, and numerous kids crumple and withdraw when their goals don't materialize. Let's use my old Wealth Creation unit as a template. It focused on these questions:

- What obstacles do you anticipate, and how will you mitigate them?

- What modest goals can you achieve and then build upon?

WHAT YOU CAN DO TOMORROW

- **Apply my Wealth Creation template to a scenario.** You can apply the template to many project-based learning prompts. Or challenge kids to engage in wild speculation about fictitious characters or historical figures.

- **Game-plan obstacles.** My late father-in-law would frequently ask, "What's the worst that can happen?" Such speculation is important. Challenge your students to do this with a goal.

- **Formulate modest goals.** Direct students to take an audacious goal and break it into smaller manageable objectives. Achieving these modest goals will build confidence and may foster a systematic approach to achieving the larger goal. It can also lead to a sense of accomplishment, even if they do not reach some of the modest objectives.

- **Apply for relevancy.** After prompting kids to apply the template to an academic scenario, instill instant relevance by challenging them to apply what they learned to one of their objectives. For example, one critical thinking standard insists that students will be able to admit mistakes and change their views when faced with good reasons to do so.

Moderate doses of negative thinking have served me well. Don't overdo optimism. Promote a balanced approach with your kids, and this honesty will keep them engaged.

MEET ME IN THE AGORA

THE PROBLEM: STUDENTS ARE RELUCTANT TO PARTICIPATE IN CLASS DISCUSSIONS

THE AGORA WAS the square in an ancient Greek city-state. It was the central meeting space where all the governing activities took place. The Greeks took democracy seriously, making participation mandatory in terms of voting and serving on massive juries that convened in the agora. Being informed was a must. The Greeks accomplished what many teachers try to achieve daily ... foster participation.

THE HACK: CREATE A GREEK AGORA IN YOUR ROOM AND FACILITATE AN ENGAGING DISCUSSION

This Hack does not involve technology. If you teach in K–12, you likely have your own classroom. If you do, rearrange the desks to create a large open space in the middle where students can congregate—an agora.

I once attended a professional development session where the presenter got us to collaborate by setting up appointments with other PD participants. She handed each of us a sheet of paper with three times listed (1 p.m., 2 p.m., and 3 p.m.). After each time was a place where a fellow participant could sign their name. You, in turn, would sign your name on their sheet, coinciding with the same time. When the presenter said, "Go meet with your 1 p.m. appointment," we would all scurry out of our seats, find our appointee, and collaborate on the prompt she had designated for 1 p.m. This was a smooth and engaging experience, and I replicate it often, even if the appointment times are only five minutes long.

For the *Meet Me in the Agora* activity, movement is crucial. When students are filling out their appointment sheets, make them do it in the agora. No one can return to their seat until their calendar is full, and no one can meet with the same person more than once. Invariably, there are a few stragglers who need appointments. This is where you may need to step in and help. You can call out, "Who still needs a 2 p.m.?" Students who have leftover time slots but no options are left on others' sheets must meet with you, their dear teacher, during that time frame. Talking with students about an engaging topic will be fun for you.

Also crucial to the success of *Meet Me in the Agora* is the formulation of three provocative prompts. Dedicate time and effort to this step. You want prompts that have many nuances to explore and where reasonable people can disagree. You also want prompts that are relevant to your students so they'll be engaged in discussing them. Conscript a few reliable students to help you craft these prompts. This will be very helpful to the class engagement level.

Once everyone has appointments and has returned to their seats, display the first prompt and direct kids out of their seats and into the agora to meet their 1 p.m. appointment, and then display a timer. I typically limit each appointment to under five minutes. Students are to remain standing (if possible) and talking until the time is up. If you're not meeting with a student, you can circulate and stir the pot if you sense that a conversation is lagging. Once time is up and everyone has returned to their seats, conduct a short debriefing session before the next prompt. Challenge kids to compliment a peer who made great points.

WHAT YOU CAN DO TOMORROW

- **Clear the middle of your room.** This is where the action will take place. If your freedom to rearrange is limited, like mine, take students to the hallway or a commons area.
- **Compose an appointment sheet.** Three appointment times are adequate.
- **Craft provocative discussion prompts.** This is the most challenging and important aspect of this Hack. Solicit students' help to create these engaging and relevant prompts.

The *Meet Me in the Agora* activity is a fun, engaging, zero-tech, and highly structured method to dramatically enhance class participation.

121

DEFINE YOUR TEACHING

THE PROBLEM: PARENTS CAN MISCHARACTERIZE YOUR TEACHING

MOST PARENTS WANT their children to learn to think critically. A great way teachers can promote such thinking is to frequently play the role of someone with a different position. When one of your kids stakes a position, you can ask questions like:

- Have you considered this alternative?

- What is a potential downside to pursuing this policy?

- When did you develop this position?

- What sources did you consult?

- Are you open to changing your mind?

These are great questions, but some, even those who claim to support critical thinking, can view them as a threat. Twenty-five hundred years ago, legendary educator Socrates was sentenced to death for asking such questions. Sadly, some educators are under siege once again. I taught World Civilization for decades in a small conservative community. We explored in great depth Buddhism, Hinduism, Daoism, and Islam. Out of the thousands of Christian students who took my class, I don't know of one who converted to any of these faiths merely because they learned about them. The good news is that epochs of academic paranoia tend to dissipate. The bad news is that while they're present, careers can be ruined and learning suffers.

THE HACK: PARTNER WITH SCHOOL LEADERS ON CONTROVERSIAL TOPICS

Javeria Salman authored a fascinating article in *The Hechinger Report* titled "Jargon May Have Turned Parents Against Social and Emotional Learning." Salman asserts that abstract jargon like Social and Emotional Learning causes problems. Opponents of such programs define such jargon in manipulative ways and inspire knee-jerk reactions in some parents. Many of these same parents, when exposed to aspects of SEL, are supportive of those specific areas. The message for teachers is that they must prevent others from defining or labeling their teaching. If you're not proactive, one of your lessons could become a target.

I'm married to a former middle school principal. She would often get inflamed phone calls from parents complaining about what a teacher did in the classroom. This would put my wife in a tough spot because the parents wanted swift justice. My wife would not make any decisions until she investigated. In most cases, the rendition she was served by the aggravated parent was not the whole picture. Other variables were involved. She always appreciated it when a teacher would collaborate with her before instructing a potentially controversial lesson. She and the teacher could then brainstorm ways to make the lesson less controversial while maintaining its impact. Most principals care a lot about learning and don't want teachers to feel muzzled. Please keep this example in mind when you plan. If a parent complains and everyone's emotions get invested, consensus becomes elusive.

WHAT YOU CAN DO TOMORROW

Here is the recipe I promote to my future teachers in my Education classes. Many future teachers are justifiably concerned about the potential for parents and students to misunderstand or misinterpret the topics being taught.

- **Investigate your school's policies.** Talk to colleagues. They are your best source. They do the same job, and they may have already navigated lesson acceptability waters. There may be a board policy on controversial topics. If so, read it.

- **Evaluate lessons.** Before each semester, highlight lessons that have the potential to be an issue.

- **Approach administration.** If you have an issue in class, your principal will hear about it. Cut this person some slack and give them a heads-up about how you plan to teach a topic before you teach it. Your principal may have great ideas on how you can improve the lesson, or they might try to talk you out of teaching it. Regardless, your principal will have a working knowledge of your lesson objectives and can better defend you and nullify outlandish claims by complainers.

- **Invite school board members to participate.** This involves risk, but it may be worth it. I would rather have a firsthand observer define my teaching than one who acquires their information from hearsay. Think about the jargon article I referenced.

Only you can decide how you'll proceed in the realm of academic freedom. Please consider these rational steps. And if you find yourself teaching in a community that doesn't support critical thinking, you can assess your options.

DEPUTIZE DEVIL'S ADVOCATES

THE PROBLEM: SOME PARENTS BELIEVE TEACHERS TRY TO UNDERMINE THEIR VALUES

Hack 70 in *Hacking Engagement Again* promotes a discussion technique called *Philosophical Chairs*. It's still hands-down my favorite way to conduct a classroom discussion. Here's a brief refresher. The teacher prompts students with a provocative dilemma, then offers students three choices:

1. Choice A represents a course of action.

2. Choice C represents the polar opposite choice.

3. Choice B is in the middle and for students who are unsure.

After students ponder a dilemma, they then physically migrate to a side of the room that is labeled A, B, or C. The teacher moderates the conversation by asking a small sample of students why they chose a certain position. If a student becomes convinced by one of their classmate's arguments, they can migrate to a different side. When this happens, and it happens often, the teacher can draw these students into the discussion by asking why they moved.

I started using *Philosophical Chairs* over a decade ago. I want to promote the deliberate way in which I moderate these discussions because it can be a template you can replicate in much of your instruction and hopefully avoid parental accusations of manipulation.

THE HACK: TRANSFORM STUDENTS INTO DEVIL'S ADVOCATES

Teachers must be careful when playing the role of devil's advocate. A student can complain to parents that you're questioning their values. Sadly, you may be doing exactly the opposite because you're helping a student learn to defend their ideas. When I play devil's advocate, I'm merely playing a role. I'm asking questions from a perspective that I may or may not endorse. Contemporary educators may be better served by allowing students to play this role. Here's how I do this under the umbrella of a *Philosophical Chairs* discussion.

Once you've prompted students with a dilemma and they've sorted themselves into various parts of the room based on their views, you start the process. Select a student and ask them to articulate their view. Allow them to pontificate for a bit, and then abruptly and enthusiastically restate and elaborate on their position. It often unfolds something like this:

> **Student A:** "High school athletes should absolutely be required to stand during *The National Anthem*. Not doing so is totally disrespectful to all of our armed service members."
>
> **Sturtevant:** "So you see this as a basic courtesy and acknowledgment to those who have sacrificed so much? Where would we be without these folks? Is that accurate?"

Always attempt to get confirmation that you're accurately portraying what they're saying. At no time do I play devil's advocate with this student. Your goal is for the student to feel heard. Then redirect to the opposite side.

> **Student C:** "Telling a student they cannot take a knee is a violation of their First Amendment freedom of expression. And taking a knee is meant to draw attention to how minorities are treated by law enforcement, not meant as a lack of support for those in the military."

Student C just assumed the role of devil's advocate. Just like with Student A, restate and elaborate Student C's position. Call on a few more students and repeat this process. Prompt any student who migrates to a new position, "Why did you move?" Prompt any students left in the middle, "Why haven't you chosen a position?" Your role will not be that of devil's advocate but of a clarifier.

WHAT YOU CAN DO TOMORROW

- **Build a foundation.** Put time and effort into facilitating an atmosphere of respect for different viewpoints. Emotions can run high in such debates.

- **Designate an engaging topic.** Some topics might be too dangerous to discuss. You may want to begin with a topic where there's less potential for post-discussion drama.

- **Create provocative dilemmas.** Epic class discussions are fueled by great prompts. Direct efforts toward crafting engaging dilemmas where reasonable people can disagree.

- **Game-plan a questioning strategy.** Invest time in speculating whom you'll call on and when. Which student might be a great devil's advocate for another student? A wonderful aspect of *Philosophical Chairs* is your role as the moderator. You're in charge, and you can step on the gas or pump the brakes. Students only talk when you call on them.

One theme I've frequently emphasized is for educators to do less and prompt students to do more. While the strategy articulated in this Hack has conflict potential, stepping away from the role of devil's advocate and allowing students to assume it is definitely worth considering.

RECONSIDER WIKIPEDIA

THE PROBLEM: IT'S HARD TO GET CONSENSUS ON WHAT CONSTITUTES A RELIABLE SOURCE

N A FASCINATING article in *UConn Today* entitled, "Cognitive Biases and Brain Biology Help Explain Why Facts Don't Change Minds," Keith Bellizzi asserts that if someone is passionate about a belief, exposing them to compelling contradictory evidence will rarely get one to abandon a cherished position. In fact, such exposure may inspire one to further dig in their heels. (For more about how to teach kids about empathy, politics, and civic responsibility, including how to recognize reputable information sources, see the book *Preventing Polarization* by Michelle Blanchet and Brian Deters.)

The implications for teachers are profound in this partisan era. Our objective is to promote reputable sources, and that's tough with contentious topics. In the not-too-distant past, information from research databases, institutions of higher learning, government agencies, or reputable

> *Crowdsourced evidence is part of this modern world.*

news outlets was rarely challenged. If you teach in a contentious environment where the motives of teachers are challenged, I have an idea for you.

THE HACK: CONSIDER WIKIPEDIA AS AN ACCEPTABLE BASE OF INFORMATION

Before any educators have a conniption about *Wikipedia*, hear me out. *Wikipedia* is a wonderful example of crowdsourcing. Crowdsourcing forms aggregate selections from vast numbers of contributors. It's the very definition of consensus. Crowdsourcing has evolved. Betting markets, another form of crowdsourcing, now rival political pollsters in terms of accuracy. *Wikipedia* has evolved too. Meghan Bogardus Cortez authored a proactive article in *EdTech* entitled "Is Wikipedia a Reliable Source? Scientists Think So." In the article, she cites studies that promote *Wikipedia* in academia and its suitability as a legitimate academic source. This is great news for me because I use *Wikipedia* daily. I'll bet you do too. I'm certain your students do as well. People have voted for *Wikipedia* with their fingertips.

If you deal with contentious subjects in your class, resource management helps. You wish that students would accept *The New York Times* as a reputable source, but you cannot bank on that. I've heard students toss out the "fake news" label to anything they disagree with. You also worry that students will start citing wild, tough-to-trace conspiracy theories from dark corners of the internet. If you start to argue with kids about the legitimacy of their sources, it might be counterproductive, as suggested by the cognitive bias article I referenced early in this Hack.

Consider using *Wikipedia* as a common source that most students can accept. This has a good chance of happening if you spend some time educating kids about crowdsourcing and how *Wikipedia* functions. If you're still old-school about your sources and *Wikipedia* is a bridge too far for you, you can always do what many of my librarian friends suggest—use *Wikipedia* as a starting point and then use the resources referenced at the end of Wikipedia posts.

WHAT YOU CAN DO TOMORROW

- **Evaluate future topics.** Your students may be presenting an oral report or writing a position paper for which they need sources. You may be supplying kids with resources and then asking them to debate a topic. Whenever you think there's potential for intense emotions or resource hijinks, consider *Wikipedia* as the primary source.

- **Create a mini-lesson about crowdsourcing.** For students to understand *Wikipedia*, it's helpful to engage them in a bit of crowdsourcing, which they usually find to be a fun experience (especially young students). They can conduct a survey at school to determine consensus on the favorite flavor of ice cream or students' favorite color. Older students can conduct surveys, too, and may also benefit from reading the *EdTech* article I mentioned. Help students learn how *Wikipedia* works.

- **Prepare a defense.** Anticipate that some parents, students, colleagues, and administrators may question your utilization of *Wikipedia*. If you find the arguments in this Hack persuasive, please use them.

Crowdsourced evidence is part of this modern world. It has the potential to supply less divisive resources in an extremely divisive academic environment.

INITIATE OSTENTATIOUS REWARD DAY

THE PROBLEM: THE CONTEMPORARY CLASSROOM DESPERATELY NEEDS A LITTLE LEVITY

I**T'S NO WONDER** that many educators are exiting the classroom. It's a tough time to be a teacher dedicated to creating an engaging learning environment where students are inspired to think critically. Contemporary classrooms desperately need a bit of levity, and this Hack can check that box.

THE HACK: CREATE AN AUDACIOUS REWARD AND DOLE IT OUT TO WORTHY RECIPIENTS ON A DESIGNATED DAY

I was watching a college football game featuring the University of Miami. One young man from the Hurricanes made a spectacular interception. As he returned to the U of M bench, his teammates enthusiastically greeted him. But then something magical happened. One of the players produced this massive gold chain and hung it around the celebrated defender's neck. Before I had time to verbalize, "What's that?" a commentator explained, "Out comes Miami's famous turn-over chain." My wheels started turning. The Miami Hurricanes looked so joyful and enthusiastic. I knew a turnover chain was in my future.

I went to the hardware store and found a roll of cheap yellow plastic chain. I purchased the correct length. I designed a cool-looking letter S on an online drawing—S for Sturtevant. I printed my cool-looking S on the color copier at school and then laminated it. I put the ensemble together and was thrilled with the result, which you can see in Image 124. Little effort or treasure was devoted to this wonderful project.

Image 124: Proudly wearing the Sturtevant Turnover Chain.

The first voyage of the Sturtevant Turnover Chain was my family's annual Super Bowl party. Many guests were awarded the chain that night. It was rewarded temporarily to invitees who:

- Brought a wonderful drink or snack
- Uttered a solid observation during the game
- Prevented any type of spill
- Paid me a compliment about the party
- Cheered loudly during the game
- Were near me when the team I was rooting for won

"Enjoy it while you have it," I warned. "Another guest will have it soon." At some point in the evening, I realized, *If fifty-year-olds enjoy wearing the Turnover Chain, kids would love it too.*

I introduced the idea to my class by showing a clip of a University of Miami football player being awarded the chain by celebratory teammates. The following Friday was designated as Ostentatious Reward Day. After we defined ostentatious and I displayed images of the Sturtevant Turnover Chain, students were then involved in the process. I asked them what they believed would warrant the temporary possession of the chain. We came up with some great prerequisites:

- Complimenting a classmate
- Wearing a nice outfit
- Being nice
- Saying something optimistic
- Giving a solid effort
- Making a great point
- Being creative

Many students wore the Turnover Chain that Friday. We only did it once. The novelty of such a tactic would wear off quickly. But it was a really fun day!

WHAT YOU CAN DO TOMORROW

- **Choose a reward.** The Turnover Chain is ostentatious and easy to construct. Please steal my idea or devote time to dreaming up something similar. If you draw blanks, you can always reward students with food. Bake a batch of your best cookies or bring in doughnuts. They'll be motivated to impress.
- **Solicit a list of reward-worthy actions or dispositions.** The criteria list was a wonderful part of the day for my class and me. This, like the *Magna Carta* in Hack 101, involves kids in the creation of an awesome class atmosphere.

As educators, we have an important reason to remain in our roles—teaching can be a lot of fun. When teachers are having fun, kids typically are as well, and that means they are engaged. We all need more days like the Ostentatious Reward Day.

EMBARK ON A FORMATIVE JOURNEY

THE PROBLEM: MANY TEACHERS AND STUDENTS THINK THAT ASSIGNING A GRADE IS THE ONLY WAY TO MOTIVATE STUDENTS

LORI SANTOS IS a psychology professor at Yale. She created a marvelous podcast called *The Happiness Lab*. I assign Episode 10, "Making the Grade," every semester in my Assessment class. This provocative podcast explores the negative impact that grades have on students. In one intriguing segment, she highlights an experiment conducted with elementary students working on anagrams. Anagrams are words where the letters have been jumbled, and one tries to identify the word by reformulating it. The elementary students in the experiment were having a grand time with this intellectual challenge. The experimenters grouped the anagrams into discrete categories: easy, moderate, and challenging. Students worked independently with no incentives and were told to solve as many as they could. The unburdened students were free to take intellectual risks, and most opted for tougher anagrams as their confidence grew.

And then the ground shifted. The researchers told the students that for the next round, their efforts would be graded. They would be awarded a grade based on how many anagrams they got right. As you can imagine, intellectual risk-taking ground to a halt. So did the joy. Students became subdued and entrenched in the lower-difficulty anagram levels.

THE HACK: CONDUCT YOUR OWN INTRINSIC FORMATIVE ASSESSMENT EXPERIMENT

Respected studies have promoted formative assessment as a powerful support to learning. I describe two examples of formative assessment experiments in this book: Hack 117 (Stage a Haiku Slam) is about a collaborative formative assessment, and Hack 120 (Meet Me in the Agora) has some collaborative aspects, but students are also asked to work independently. Consider creating a collaborative formative assessment in which students have a fair amount of independence.

Options for a collaborative effort may include:

- Creating a physical demonstration
- Putting together a slide presentation
- Performing a skit
- Building a model

Options for an independent effort may include:

- Solving a problem
- Working through a puzzle
- Creating an artifact
- Drawing a comic

Keep this learning activity contained in one class period; this is not homework. Students navigate both my haiku and agora activities in roughly twenty minutes. In the midst of these activities, a few students ask, "Are we getting a grade for this?" and I respond, "Don't worry about that. I'll take care of you. I promise." While this is not satisfactory to my small cadre of gradeaholics, I stand by my elusiveness and keep smiling and nodding.

When most teachers think of a formative assessment, they conjure a quick barometric check. The formative assessments I promote in this Hack require more time, effort, and intellectual risk. They also become the central learning activities of the day.

Some teachers may be uncomfortable with the idea of spending so much class time on a formative assessment. Some may also be concerned about the lack of a grade motivator. Remember, this is an experiment. My question was: "Would students be engaged if no grades were attached?" The answer was a resounding "Yes!"

WHAT YOU CAN DO TOMORROW

- **Design a collaborative formative assessment.** The haiku prompt helps students demonstrate an understanding of advanced concepts. Consider the collaborative ideas promoted earlier in this Hack.

- **Create a prompt where students work independently.** The *Meet Me in the Agora* prompt inspires students to speculate and troubleshoot. Consider the ideas for independent work promoted earlier in this Hack.

- **Observe.** Watch your kids during this experiment. While I'll concede that my observations aren't objective, I did notice an unmistakable increase in energy and volume. These are certainly engagement indicators.

- **Debrief with students.** Ask them what they thought. I predict that most comments will be complimentary.

- **Evaluate effectiveness.** The summative assessment results on the concepts I was formatively assessing improved from the previous semesters! While it's difficult to prove a causal relationship between a learning activity and a summative assessment result, it's safe to say that students were engaged by these fun formative assessments and still hit their learning targets.

Teachers often think of formative assessments as supplementing a learning activity. But what if the formative assessment is the learning activity? Researchers learned a lot about student motivation and engagement with their low-stakes anagram experiment. Perhaps, you could do something similar.

FLIP A PODCAST

THE PROBLEM: PODCASTS
ARE UNDERUTILIZED

MY FIRST YEAR of teaching was a blur. In addition to intense deadline pressure, I was also plagued by a lack of knowledge about diverse ways to deliver content. I taught the way I was taught to teach. My history professors and my former social studies teachers in K–12 would have me read something outside of class, and then they would talk about it in class. Some were better at lecturing than others. This was and is an extremely passive learning template. My first year as a teacher, I'm embarrassed to admit, I tried to do much the same. My students got tired of listening to me, and I got tired of talking, but I didn't have much knowledge about alternative approaches. So when the last day of school finally rolled around, I knew, moving forward, that I had to change.

In the decades that followed, I was always game to try new methods of content delivery.

I was particularly motivated when I first learned about flipped presentations. You can assign students an existing YouTube video, or you can create one. It didn't take long for me to become a flipped-video-producing machine. I loved the contemporary *When in Rome* feel of assigning a video. After all, students seemed inclined to watch videos constantly by default. That's what they do when they have downtime. Flipped presentations capitalize on this disposition. I'm still a huge fan, but I took a quantum leap a few years ago when I started to assign podcasts regularly. Just like with a video, you can flip a podcast. Assign one to your students as an alternative to an in-class lecture. Students can listen to their homework and then apply the lesson in class the next day.

THE HACK: ASSIGN A FLIPPED PODCAST TO STUDENTS

This may seem like a no-brainer, but few of my students report that podcasts are used in their classes. That's too bad because podcasts offer a flexibility that in-person lectures and flipped video presentations cannot touch—consumption flexibility. While flipped video presentations offer time and place consumption freedom, you still have to sit down and watch. Podcasts can be consumed while you drive, mow the lawn, work out, and, unfortunately, with earphones at the family dinner table.

WHAT YOU CAN DO TOMORROW

- **Find a great podcast.** This is crucial. If you assign a long, boring podcast, you'll poison the well. Good luck assigning another. I try to set a limit of thirty minutes and fall in the fifteen- to twenty-minute sweet spot. Spotify and Apple Podcasts are two prominent platforms. One could also conduct a basic search. Most podcasts have show pages with embedded sound files.

- **Create an engaging way for students to respond to the podcast.** It's important to hold kids accountable. Some educators shy away from flipped presentations because of the accountability issue. They are concerned that students won't watch or won't be attentive. Make sure to follow up the podcast with questions about the program. It'll be obvious whether they were attentive or not. This can also be a written reflection that accompanies the podcast prompt or a small-group discussion when class reconvenes.

Podcasts are a perfect blend of enhanced content delivery and student mobility. And, podcasts are underutilized by educators. This is one way you can become the forward-leaning tech all-star of your department and engage your kids at the same time.

PROMOTE A PROCESS

THE PROBLEM: MOST STUDENTS DON'T HAVE A CREATIVE PROCESS

T HE OLDER I get, the worse I sleep. The good news is that there's consensus on positive steps one can take to set up a good night's sleep. Researchers refer to taking these actions as *creating good sleep hygiene*. The list includes ideas such as:

- Reduce the amount of light in your bedroom.

- Don't watch stressful shows late in the evening.

- If you're awake for more than fifteen minutes, get out of bed.

- Don't nap during the day (I fail at this directive almost every twenty-four hours).

These are common-sense approaches, but sound sleep can be elusive. You can do everything right and still toss and turn. Interestingly enough, I've learned that obsessing over sleep is my biggest disruptor.

In many ways, chasing sleep is like chasing creativity. You cannot will yourself into being creative, but you can optimize conditions that may encourage it. The trick is to identify those catalytic conditions and attempt to recreate them. Unlike sleep, however, there isn't consensus on steps one can take to be creative. Your creative template is probably as unique as your fingerprints.

THE HACK: CHALLENGE KIDS TO MAKE YOUR ROOM A MORE CREATIVE PLACE

Nothing is more engaging than being submerged in the creative process. But chasing this state can be as elusive as trying to fall asleep. It may help to start by providing an example of a creative template. As a personal example, here's my creative process for writing the Hacks in this book. The process typically took twenty-four hours. Here's how such a non-teaching day unfolded:

6:00 – 6:15 a.m.	Focus only on the title and the Problem.
6:15 – 9:00 a.m.	Exercise me and my dogs. Read the news.
9:00 – 10:00 a.m.	Compose the description of the Problem.
10:00 – 11:00 a.m.	Eat breakfast.
11:00 a.m. – 12:00 p.m.	Create the Hack and one-sentence bullets in the What You Can Do Tomorrow section.
12:00 – 3:00 p.m.	Daily chores
3:00 – 4:00 p.m.	Fill in the blank portions of the Hack. By 4:00 p.m., I generally had between six hundred and eight hundred words and a freshly minted Hack.
4:00 – 10:00 p.m.	Whatever the heck I want.

There are long gaps between periods of productivity. I do all kinds of things during these gaps, but I try not to think about the Hack at all during these lulls.

After you give students your example, challenge them to create a similar process. Ask them to recall a creation event. It can be a song they wrote, a game they invented, a model they built, a story they crafted, an athletic skill they mastered, or an instrument they finally learned to play. Give students a blank, twenty-four-hour template and have them map out everything they can remember about the day this event occurred. They may not remember much. If that's the case, encourage them to speculate.

Ask them to share their creative event day portraits in small groups where they address these questions:

- Did you create in stages or take breaks, or did you invest totally from start to finish?

- Did you listen to music?

- What were your feelings during the creation process?

- Did you go back and change anything?

After groups have analyzed their creative event day portraits, challenge them to transport ideas from their portraits into the academic realm. Have them address these prompts:

- Were the creative portraits in your group similar?

- How can I take one thing from what I love to do and apply it to homework from this class?

- How can our classroom be altered physically to enhance creative productivity?

- How can our classroom procedures be altered to enhance creative productivity?

Have students share some of the interesting ideas that emerged from this proactive session.

WHAT YOU CAN DO TOMORROW

- **Provide an example.** Create a portrait of a creative day you're willing to share. Tell the twenty-four-hour story about when you created a viral social media post, bench pressed three hundred pounds, or, if you're totally old-school, scrapbooked from daybreak till dusk.

- **Create a blank twenty-four-hour template.** This is where students will depict their creative day. Many will struggle to write much, and that's okay.

- **Decide on a sharing mechanism.** It's important for students to publicly broadcast their classroom transformation ideas. A virtual bulletin board will work.

While you aren't likely to install a state-of-the-art sound system or meditation pods in your classroom, your students will probably come up with an idea that they like and you're willing to try. Regardless, getting kids to think about the creative process is worthwhile, even if you don't come up with many actionable ideas.

EXPLORE AN INTERACTIVE TIMELINE

THE PROBLEM: MANY STUDENT-BUILT MODELS ARE NOT ACCURATE OR INTERACTIVE

I LOVE READING A book at bedtime that sweeps me away from my intense daily focus. I'm currently reading a great one—*A Short History of Nearly Everything* by Bill Bryson. It's a wonder-producing science book. I navigate a few pages each night before I nod off. The fact that the book puts me to sleep doesn't seem like an endorsement, but endorsing the book is my intention. I recently read a story in it that inspired this Hack. Bryson was explaining how the models of the solar system on elementary classroom walls are wildly inaccurate. The planets' size proportions are way off, and so are the distances between planets. He acknowledges that accurately modeling the solar system on a poster or a textbook illustration is darned near impossible. Okay, Bryson—you got me thinking.

Another contributor to this Hack is my observation that many state learning standards call for students to build models that demonstrate complex ideas or phenomena. These are solid objectives that embody the spirit of higher-level thinking. Many times when kids respond to such prompts, however, the models they construct are like the poster of the solar system that I used to gaze at in third grade—they aren't very accurate and are rarely interactive.

THE HACK: PROMPT STUDENTS TO CREATE AN INTERACTIVE TIMELINE

As a former history teacher, I'd occasionally challenge students to create a timeline. Placing events in order is important, and graphically organizing ideas promotes understanding. But I was rarely impressed with what students created. Their timelines were generally drab and sparse. The problem was not a lack of creativity; the issue was with me. Your humble narrator was not issuing an inspiring timeline prompt, nor was I supplying them with the tools to make their models pop.

Image 128: An example of how I used the Knight Lab StoryMap software to demonstrate five transformational events in my early life.

And this, dear reader, is where Knight Lab's StoryMap makes a dramatic appearance. This wonderful tool was created at Northwestern University. Your students just sign in with their Gmail accounts and start creating. The site saves what they've done, and your kids can easily acquire shareable links to their projects. This helpful feature provides presentation flexibility. When it's time to present their timelines, students can do it in person or virtually. When students create a story map timeline, they can insert images, links, and even videos, all of which make this timeline interactive. On the left side is a map that shows the place. This feature is powered by Google Maps. On the right side of the story map are the information, links, images, and videos that students insert. Image 128 shows the example I used to demonstrate the platform. You can use any other presentation software as well.

A Knight Lab StoryMap is perfect for any grade level or any subject. Your elementary students can create a timeline for a book they're reading or create a family history. You can challenge science students to create a story map about the receding Ice Age or about the scientific breakthroughs of the European Enlightenment. Please consider adding one more variable. Entice your students to include personal experiences. This will also ramp up interactivity and engagement. In my Education Technology class, we created a story map about the evolution of virtual learning. I wanted three timeline markers from the study material and three from their experiences. Here's the prompt:

From the study material:

- List three significant concepts from the resources. Research when these ideas were created and how they evolved.

From your experiences:

- Your first memory of using a computer

- Your first memory of using a cellphone

- The most impactful way you used technology when you were a student

WHAT YOU CAN DO TOMORROW

- **Create a personal example.** This will help you learn the platform and provide your students with a solid example. Creating a five-marker timeline on how you became their teacher is one idea.

- **Contemplate a topic.** You want an engaging topic and one where kids can insert some personal experience. For my Ice Age suggestion, I asked them to demonstrate when they have been in different types of terrain. They could display a vacation when they were in the mountains and one where they were in a flat area.

- **Formulate presentation groups.** Students having to sit through similar timeline presentations from classmates in a large class would be tedious for everyone. Perhaps offer a handful of topics and then have students present to small groups of classmates.

Your state probably wants your students to build models to demonstrate complex concepts. Take this a step forward and challenge kids to create interactive models that include their personal experiences. Knight Lab's StoryMap may be the perfect vehicle.

LEVERAGE A LEARNING EXPERIENCE

THE PROBLEM: TEACHERS OFTEN FAIL TO ASK FOR STUDENT HELP IN LESSON DESIGN

R ECENTLY, I WAS navigating a lesson on project-based learning with my education students. We were creating PBL prompts, and we were striving to include these seven elements:

1. Anchor (the subject matter in the unit being studied)

2. Task

3. Directions

4. Student choice

5. Student inquiry

6. Teacher coaching

7. Public presentation

Prior to students creating their PBL prompts, I assigned a profound reflection activity. They were to recall a powerful learning experience—in or out of the school setting. They could cite when a coach helped them master an athletic skill or when their piano teacher freed them to improvise.

After they chose their experience, they were to create a three-panel comic strip. This strip would incorporate as many of the seven PBL elements as possible. They could certainly draw a rough sketch, but I had my students create their comic strip with a neat platform called StoryBoard That. All my students screenshotted their creations and put them on a communal slideshow. We had a lot of fun reviewing them.

Before I prompted them to create a comic strip, I created an example and shared it for guidance. Mine came from third grade, which, for me, was half a century ago! That's the power of an engaging lesson. Few students can remember what they did in class last week, let alone last year. Our teacher prompted us to redraw the boundaries of the state of Ohio. We could draw them any way we wanted, but we had to justify what we created. Even as a young guy, I was struck by the fact that the eastern part of Ohio is hilly and the western part is flat. So I cut Ohio in half—Hilly Ohio and Flat Ohio. I was excited to show my parents.

My students' examples of past learning were as powerful for them as mine was for me. This exercise helped put them in the right frame of mind to create their PBL prompts.

THE HACK: ASK STUDENTS TO MINE AN IDEA FROM A POWERFUL LEARNING EXPERIENCE

If you teach very young students, their example of profound learning may be like when their mom taught them to tie their shoes. You would certainly not ask young students to apply the seven elements of PBL to their example. Instead, ask them three questions:

1. What did you do?

2. Why was it engaging?

3. How did it impact you?

If you like my three-panel comic strip idea, you can use these questions to inspire the panels. (For more about how to teach higher-level thinking with comics and visual storytelling, see the book *Hacking Graphic Novels* by Shveta V. Miller.) After students have their examples and you review them as a class, the fun can really start. Display upcoming topics or lessons, and challenge students to choose one and consider it in light of the profound learning experience they just shared. Prompt them to pull one idea or element from their example or one element from one of their classmates' examples and transpose it onto a future class topic. In other words: Take a learning scenario that worked for you or a classmate in the past and apply it to the future.

This will be a huge challenge for most kids. Don't be upset if you get just a few workable ideas. And you certainly have veto power. These ideas may be jackpots, and your students will be impressed that you respect them enough to ask for their input.

WHAT YOU CAN DO TOMORROW

- **Produce a three-panel comic promoting a deep learning experience from your past.** This helped give my students a bit of direction. It also familiarized me with the StoryBoard That platform.

- **Ask kids to recall a powerful learning experience.** Incorporate the three basic questions listed earlier and decide how they'll produce and display their comic strips.

- **Evaluate future topics.** What upcoming lessons will be perfect for student manipulation? You can also turn this into a regular activity, such as once a month.

Diversifying the way in which students can demonstrate learning is a good thing. Encouraging students to be involved in lesson planning is a good thing. Throughout this process, you may be exposed to ideas that will profoundly influence your future lesson planning.

MANIFEST A ROOM FULL OF COHORTS

THE PROBLEM: MANY STUDENT GROUPS DISBAND BEFORE THEY LEARN TO EFFECTIVELY COLLABORATE

MANY YEARS AGO, I had lunch every day with a cohort of male colleagues. After a time, we claimed a table in the center of the teacher's lounge and started eating there every day at noon. We called our little piece of public property *The Round Table*. We avoided any school talk and mostly stuck to analyzing a recent sporting event or complaining about how unfairly our wives treated us. Yes, we were all pampered. These complaints were not real. Over time, we got to know each other well, and our conversations became remarkably efficient, productive, and enjoyable. I miss those guys and those lunches.

This past semester, I became determined to enhance peer collaboration in

> *A cohort setup gives you ready-made groups that already have experience collaborating.*

my Education classes, so I created cohort groups. (I'm not sure why I love the word cohort.) I chose my cohorts randomly by arranging students alphabetically by first name. I then created groups of four or five. These cohorts collaborated on various tasks for several weeks. And then, I broke out the *Random Name Generator* and re-sorted. Many students were reluctant to leave their established cohort—a wonderful sign of the effectiveness of this student engagement Hack.

THE HACK: CREATE SMALL COHORT GROUPS IN YOUR CLASS

My original thought on creating the cohorts was to facilitate participatory, engaging, and collaborative small-group discussion. Cohorts worked perfectly for this. What I didn't anticipate was how much I'd utilize these semi-permanent groupings in the pursuit of other objectives.

During class, I often toss out a problem that students need to solve and then direct them to present their products or ideas to their classmates.

Many of the Hacks I promote in this book create such a scenario. A cohort setup gives you ready-made groups that already have experience collaborating. Issue a prompt, direct them to their cohorts, and give them a presentation deadline. This has worked well for me, and I can envision the same for you, regardless of the grade you teach.

But please don't limit the focus of your cohorts to only academic prompts. In Hack 101, the *Magna Carta*, they worked on classroom procedures. This was the first day of class, and it can act as a great breaking-in exercise for your newly formed cohorts. In fact, I plan to expand the scope of my cohorts' efforts. I love the idea of creating standing groups. In other words, each cohort, in addition to other prompts I give them, can focus on one area of the way the class functions and maintain that focus for a period of time until I switch topics or rotate group members. Here are some topic ideas:

1. The Student Morale Cohort

2. The Assessment Cohort

3. The Student Workload Cohort

4. The Student Engagement Cohort

5. The Classroom Procedures Cohort

If you have twenty-five students and five cohort groups of five, these can be your standing topics. They focus on their assigned topics, which are rotated every nine weeks. These cohorts can meet briefly each week, collaborate about how your classroom is functioning, and then provide you with invaluable advice.

WHAT YOU CAN DO TOMORROW

- **Develop a lesson on highly functional groups.** Emelina Minero wrote a solid article in *Edutopia* entitled "Group Work That Works" in January of 2019. She addresses topics like member roles and making introverts feel welcome.

- **Decide on sorting.** This is an essential issue. Your sorting can be random, like mine, or you can sort based on a factor. You can mix or match introverts and extroverts. You may give students a learning-style preference survey and then mix accordingly. Decide how large you want your groups to be and how long they'll remain intact. One additional important factor is to decide how you'll react if kids in a cohort don't get along.

- **Explore cohort missions.** I love the idea of the small-group virtual discussion. Strategize how you can make this happen. But small-group discussion is merely scratching the cohort potential. Consider all the class-room management ideas articulated in this Hack.

A cohort group is a great way to encourage and facilitate student collaboration. Individual accountability is not lost in a cohort and may even be enhanced. Cohorts can also address topics where no assessment is involved. The relationships forged in groups can be engaging, powerful, and lasting.

HONE YOUR NONVERBAL PRESENTATION SKILLS

THE PROBLEM: WE AREN'T ALWAYS COGNIZANT OF HOW WE COME ACROSS

LOVE PRACTICING WHAT I preach every time I interact with students. Teachers, including me, broadcast at least as much—and generally more—than we receive. This Hack perfectly complements Hack 73 in *Hacking Engagement Again*, "Listen to Students with Your Entire Body."

I became acutely aware of the importance of nonverbal presentation signals once I started working with future educators. At the beginning of the semester when they march up in front of the room and face their peers for the first time, many of them are so nervous. Typically, they speak rapidly, don't make much eye contact, and often face the door or window, looking for an escape hatch. Getting comfortable in front of students is an essential and stressful rite of passage for every educator. If you're uptight or unconfident, you're a goner. So, I entice my sometimes-reluctant students up in front of their peers early and then often. Even though their classmates in a college Education class are a far more forgiving audience than the rows of rowdy middle schoolers they'll eventually face, it still promotes confidence. I love to watch their confidence grow as the semester unfolds.

THE HACK: COMPILE A NONVERBAL SIGNALS INVENTORY

For my future teachers, I created a rubric for their classmates to complete while they're presenting. If they ace all eight criteria, they're powerfully engaging their audience. Please steal my list or make one based on your priorities.

Non-Verbal Signal Inventory	Well Done 2	Present but Needs Work 1	Not Present 0
I made eye contact with a majority of the students.			
I smiled often.			
I spoke at the proper pace.			
I moved around and faced numerous students.			
I used welcoming hand gestures that weren't hyper.			
I didn't look back at the screen (reading notes) for extended periods.			
I projected confidence.			
I projected enthusiasm.			

Total Score _____ out of 16 possible points

Image 131: A self-assessment rubric.

My student presenters also fill out an identical self-assessment rubric (see Image 131) when they're finished. It's fascinating for them to learn from their peers' evaluations. There are typically surprises.

WHAT YOU CAN DO TOMORROW

- **Rearrange your room.** I teach in two classrooms, neither of which is conducive to me making a favorable nonverbal impact on my students. Each room has three long rows of tables that form a significant barrier between the students and me. What's more, because the tables all touch, movement is relegated to circling the outside of the room. These rooms are not my classrooms like when I taught in K–12. Hence, I'm not empowered to move the furniture. Hopefully, you have that freedom. If so, sit at various student desks and imagine yourself presenting in front of the class. Rearrange your furniture so you eliminate some barriers between you and your students in a way that facilitates movement through the heart of your classroom. I liked keeping the central part of my room open.

- **Compose your nonverbal signals inventory.** Use some or all of my nonverbal signals; engaging audiences is one of my strengths, and it can be yours too.

- **Find an evaluator.** This is a crucial step. My students are often surprised by how their classmates assess them. A natural candidate to assess you is a colleague who also wishes to improve their presentations. You can assess each another. A courageous option is to deputize a couple of trusted students and have them assess you. I love this option.

- **Record yourself.** If you are committed to growing in this important realm, film yourself practicing a presentation at home. This can be the ultimate humbling experience. You may see all types of signals that you weren't aware that you broadcast.

You may be undermining student engagement if you're broad-casting unintended nonverbals. Your words are important, but they won't have much impact unless they're coupled with confident actions.

ELIMINATE GAPS

THE PROBLEM: STUDENTS ARE ANXIOUS ABOUT THEIR LEARNING GAPS

S OMETIMES, WRITING BOOKS like this seems like a confession. I don't want to come off as self-promotional; I want to frequently highlight my shortcomings, my mistakes, and how I know I can improve. I try to be the same with my students—as I highlight in Hack 141. This confession, however, is a sad one. I failed high school chemistry. It was my junior year, and I was wrapped up in being cool, being a slacker, and being social. This was back in the late 1970s, and the movement to diversify instruction was still in its infancy, so I don't blame my teacher. It was a one-size-fits-all learning environment era, and in Chemistry, I didn't fit. Aside from my overconfident exterior, I was anxious. I had no confidence in that class, so my learning gaps in chemistry were wide and deep. This class was the least engaging educational experience of my life. I hated walking in every day.

Thankfully, today, we encourage educators to identify learning gaps and then eliminate them. It's a tall order, though. In a class of twenty-five students, you may have twenty-five distinct learning gaps. These twenty-five unique gaps may call for twenty-five creative remedies. Nevertheless, eliminating learning gaps is a necessary objective, and I'm glad it's a part of modern teaching. Student engagement simply cannot materialize if kids aren't relaxed and confident. This Hack offers an approach to identifying and eliminating learning gaps that perhaps you hadn't considered.

THE HACK: COMMISSION STUDENTS TO HELP IDENTIFY AND ELIMINATE THEIR LEARNING GAPS

Recently, I was asked to teach a new class. My department head convinced me to take on Adolescent and Young Adult (middle and high school) Curriculum and Design. My boss said, "Teach it how you want. You have all of that experience at the high school level. And also, see if there's a new text you'd like to use." I spent the better part of a summer planning lessons and evaluating texts. Julie Dirksen wrote a spectacular supplemental text called *Design for How People Learn* in November 2011. She combines extensive knowledge of pedagogy with her experience in professional development in the private sector. This book is conversational, funny, easy to read, profound, and full of clever illustrations. Every educator should consider reading it.

She frequently references learning gaps. Her approach is for learners to identify their own. She also makes an important distinction between knowledge and skill gaps. Not only can students help identify gaps, but they can also play an active role in filling them. Several years ago, I had my high school students compose a five-paragraph persuasive essay. Many struggled with this because of undiagnosed learning gaps. Here's how I wish I would have proceeded before issuing this prompt:

Step 1: I wish I had administered a pre-assessment that measured content knowledge and assessed confidence in mastering certain skills, but it's not too late for you to do so. See Image 132.

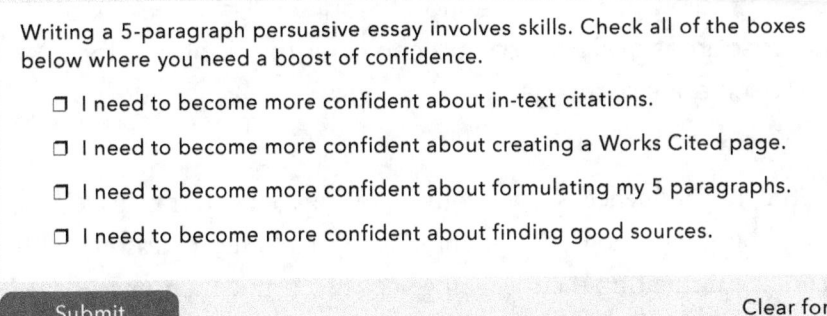

Image 132: A pre-assessment of students' self-confidence about their essay skills.

Step 2: Formulate gap-based collaboration groups. Obviously, if only one student cited a specific gap, then you would work with that kid. But several students struggled with the same skills. It would have been easy to group these kids if only I'd known, and it would have been logistically helpful, too, because a portion of the class could have been devoted to a specific gap. If many students had indicated that they struggled with confidence in many areas, they could have navigated a gap-filling circuit. For this prompt, we used *The Purdue Owl Writing Lab* as a go-to resource. Each collaboration group had access to a great skill intervention resource from this site.

Step 3: Reissue the pre-assessment. Did their confidence improve in terms of content and skills? In other words, were gaps filled?

WHAT YOU CAN DO TOMORROW

- **Create a pre-assessment.** A spreadsheet can work great. Assess students' knowledge and skills. Create a form that you can issue twice—before the learning activity and then after.
- **Find gap-elimination resources.** Your gap-filling intentions will be meaningless if you don't devote time

to finding great intervention resources. Have a bank of resources available so you can offer the right one for each anticipated gap.

Student confidence is a prerequisite to engagement. If kids feel anxious about their knowledge or abilities, your wonderful lesson will be opaque. Eliminating their learning gaps can prime their pumps.

133

GET THEM TO DRAW AGAIN

THE PROBLEM: MANY STUDENTS ARE RELUCTANT TO DRAW

M Y FAVORITE HACK in my first book on engagement is about drawing. Hack 15 is titled "Turn Your Students Into Five-Year-Olds." The objective of that Hack was to inspire students to be creative. I love the five-year-old reference because most kids at that age are less inhibited, especially when it comes to drawing. While this is an anecdotal observation, I'm confident most educators will agree that as many kids age, they become less confident in their drawing skills. But your kids absolutely should be drawing regardless of their artistic paranoia. It's a wonderful way to express oneself. This Hack is different because here, I seek to provide a powerful option instead of pen and paper.

THE HACK: PROMPT STUDENTS TO CREATE AN ONLINE DRAWING THAT DEMONSTRATES A COMPLEX IDEA

One fateful evening, I was doing some last-minute lesson planning. The next day, I planned to challenge my students to do some old-school drawing—as in drawing on a piece of paper. I was unsettled because the previous semester when I had issued this prompt, a number of my students, most of whom were in their late teens, drew stick figures. They sleepwalked through the prompt, which asked them to demonstrate a complex topic with a drawing. Granted, there were some solid submissions, but I don't think the lesson was engaging for most, nor did it inspire deep learning. It didn't help that I had one kid who was like Michelangelo. Everybody's drawing looked elementary next to hers. So most kids put forth minimal effort.

By accident, I hit "File" then "New" in my Google Drive, and Google Drawings materialized as an option. I'd heard of Google Drawings, but I'd never tried one. I quickly found a tutorial, and I was hooked within minutes. The next two hours flew by. I produced an awesome drawing. I knew exactly how I would change my prompt to include drawing as the creation vehicle. I couldn't wait to get to school the next morning.

Online drawing has become a staple of my instruction ever since. I've prompted high school students, college students, and graduate students to craft a drawing. When I ask students to name their favorite activity, online drawing gets the most first-place votes. Here's what I've learned about using this amazing tool:

- **Make your drawing prompt an online activity.** You'll learn a lot about drawing in the process and be in a better position to mentor students. Your drawing will also serve as a powerful example. In my Education Technology class, I gave a Google Drawings assignment for students to employ images, shapes, and text boxes to create a prompt about a twenty-first-century theme. My drawing even contained a hyperlink where students were instructed to submit their drawings. In my drawing, I favored PNG images, many of which have transparent

backgrounds. Such images make your drawing look cool
because pictures are layered on top of one another.

- **Demonstrate and then play.** Find a short online drawing
  tutorial that you can display. After each feature or tactic
  is demonstrated, pause the video and challenge the kids
  to practice it on their devices. Leave ample playtime at
  the end of the period where students can start creating
  their drawings.

- **Include peer presentations.** Create a communal place for
  students to post their drawings. I had them present their
  drawings in small groups. Each group then selected a
  favorite, and these drawing all-stars then presented their
  masterpieces to the entire class.

- **Give kids the old-school option.** Some kids love to draw on
  paper, and we don't want to discourage them by requiring
  an online drawing. I would generally have one or two students who would choose this option, and I welcomed it.

WHAT YOU CAN DO TOMORROW

- **Learn online drawing.** This is an important step.
  What you select will educate you and your students.
  Select a relatively short one.

- **Decide on the concept.** The objective is for kids to
  take a complex idea, like a twenty-first-century skill, and
  then demonstrate it on a one-page drawing. I'm certain
  your curriculum is rife with ideas.

- **Create the prompt via your own online drawing.**
  This was fun and helpful. Please act on this suggestion,
  as students will love it.

- **Create a communal display.** Students need to post their drawings so classmates can see them. I've used a landing pad where students can submit a link to their creations. You want students to show off what they create, like the enthusiastic five-year-olds they once were.

Engaging students with drawing offers a powerful path to youthful creative courage.

134

TRANSFORM A RUBRIC

THE PROBLEM: MOST RUBRICS AREN'T USER-FRIENDLY

J ENNIFER GONZALEZ IS a celebrated author and podcaster. In 2019, she produced a spectacular episode entitled "Rubric Repair: 5 Changes That Get Results." I assign this podcast every semester in my Assessment class. It transformed the way I teach. You can find the show and episode at cultofpedagogy.com.

Most rubrics aren't user-friendly. They're too confusing, too long, too boring, and are darned elusive because while they strive to be objective measures, most fall short. Teachers can empathize with students who are perplexed by rubrics because we're subjected to state evaluation rubrics, which can be mazes of complexity. I opened the Ohio Teacher Evaluation System Rubric, went to the *Accomplished* column, and scrolled down. Not only is the rubric long and complex, but it's also elusive. I immediately spotted these highly subjective phrases:

- *The teacher initiates effective ...*
- *The teacher exemplifies ...*
- *The teacher consistently pursues ...*

- *The teacher intentionally and strategically selects ...*

What is meant by initiates, effective, exemplifies, consistently, intentionally, and strategically? I did well on my teacher evaluations, but not because I internalized the rubric. Instead, I found it mystifying. We can do better.

THE HACK: BUILD A USER-FRIENDLY RUBRIC THAT INSPIRES LEARNING, CREATIVITY, AND COLLABORATION

Most rubrics are built for the evaluator and not the student. In Gonzalez's podcast, one option she promotes is the single-point rubric. A single-point rubric is like a to-do list, and the criteria are like jobs to complete. There's space to the right and left of each criterion for feedback. I immediately created one and then issued it for an online drawing prompt. Image 134 shows two of the nine criteria from my rubric creation.

I satisfied this criteria and I'm prepared to defend this choice when I collaborate with Mr. Sturtevant.	Criteria: Place an X in the space on the left if you satisfied the criteria. Place an X in the space on the right if you did not.	I did not satisfy this criterion and I'm prepared to make revisions.
	My Google Drawing includes 3 images with transparent backgrounds. These images support the learning target.	
	My Google Drawing includes 3 text boxes. The narratives describe the learning activity.	

Image 134: A single-point rubric for a Google Drawings prompt.

Before you guide students to apply a rubric to their work, have them apply it to samples. These samples can be from peers, but you'll get more honesty if you distribute anonymous past student submissions. Don't indicate whether you think that work is good or not. Let kids evaluate and then see if there is any consensus. This *Kid as Evaluator* exercise is easily facilitated with this user-friendly rubric. Such an endeavor also inspires great clarity when your students go into creation mode.

I was concerned that giving students such a *just-the-facts-Ma'am* rubric would not inspire them to be creative. That was not the case; their drawings were advanced and creative. My pedestrian theory is that this user-friendly rubric freed them.

My final pitch for such a rubric is how it demands collaboration. There's still ambiguity in my rubric. The phrases *support the learning target* and *describe the learning target* are inherently subjective. Your rubrics probably have ambiguity as well. You'll want to flesh out those variables both before and after assessment—and that's where collaboration comes in. Explain the rubric, guide students to self-assess, and then you can assess. Get together with kids and compare. The empty text boxes on the sides of each criterion provide space to add brief comments. You can expand on these comments when you meet with each student.

When I employed this rubric, I was pleased that we had an overwhelming consensus when it came to my evaluations and their self-evaluations. These students knew exactly where they were going with this prompt. I'm confident this rubric played a big part in that clarity.

WHAT YOU CAN DO TOMORROW

- **Consider a single-point rubric for your next prompt.** More complex rubrics may be appropriate in many cases, but consider the clarity of the single-point template. If you need a bit more sophistication but still want your rubric to be single-point, you can give more weight to important criteria. Just make sure you explain this to kids. When you do this, expose them to a weighted grade calculator so they understand how their score unfolds.

- **Designate student examples for rubric application.** Student samples from previous semesters will work well. If you don't have any, be sure to hang onto a few from this student batch of submissions; this way, you'll have a collection from which to choose moving forward.

- **Debrief students.** When you evaluate student performance, ask students what they thought of the rubric. Did the rubric help guide their creation process? Did it inspire them to be more or less creative?

Rubrics need to be user-friendly. A single-point rubric may not be the best evaluation tool for all your prompts, but you should certainly give it a try. If students become engaged with your rubric, their submissions should be awesome.

MAKE ASSESSMENT ENGAGING

THE PROBLEM: TEST ANXIETY UNDERMINES STUDENT LEARNING

KNEW THAT TEST anxiety was a thing when I was teaching K–12, but I didn't realize how big a thing it was until I started teaching Assessment to education students. At the beginning of each semester, I prompt them to share their worst assessment experiences with their neighbors. The room erupts in passionate conversation in the wake of that prompt. It's easy to talk about *when you've been done wrong* by a test. Typical student assessment abuse scenarios include:

- *I ran out of time, and the teacher took my test.*

- *I was surprised by what was on the test. We didn't go over that stuff.*

- *I wrote a great extended response, but the teacher was obsessed with grammatical errors.*

- *I knew my stuff, but when I got the test, I just froze.*

Those student assessment abuse scenarios cause a lot of anxiety. The good news is that if your assessments are a series of collaborations with students, you can alleviate much of their anxiety.

You may be thinking, *Hold on. This is supposed to be a book about engaging students in learning. Why is he talking about assessment?* Assessment, in general, and collaborative assessment,

> **The logistical headache of assessment revision is worth it.**

in particular, have massive engagement potential. In *Hacking Student Learning Habits*, Elizabeth Jorgensen explains process-based assessment, which teaches and engages students in feedback literacy, a system of ongoing assessment throughout projects and lessons. This makes assessment engaging and habitual.

THE HACK: TRANSFORM ASSESSMENT INTO A CONFIDENCE-BUILDING PROCESS INSTEAD OF AN ANXIETY-PRODUCING EVENT

Step 1: Involve students in the assessment creation process. Just like with the *Magna Carta* Hack, where students help create classroom procedures, you are erecting guardrails by giving students rational options, each of which you must approve. In the case of creating an assessment, you can choose the learning targets while giving students some say.

You might prompt students like this:

Collaborate in your group and attempt to reach a consensus on the following:

- *Of the five learning targets we covered in this unit, rank them in order of importance. If we can gain some consensus in terms of rank order, each target will then be weighted accordingly on the assessment.*

- *Of the five learning targets we covered, what would be the best type of prompt for you to demonstrate learning?*

Step 2: Promote revision. Many educators balk at this directive. There's a feeling among some teachers that this represents an unfair advantage or encourages students not to take the first attempt seriously. These arguments may have merit, but I'm more persuaded by those who point to the incredible learning experience of fixing or improving. This improvement will take place in partnership with you, which will nurture stronger bonds with kids. These collaboration sessions can be highly engaging and pave the way for increasing student confidence. The logistical headache of assessment revision is worth it. And finally, allowing for assessment revision will likely reduce anxiety. Students can then relax and demonstrate learning.

Step 3: Empower students to help you improve your assessments. After the assessment is over and students have received their results, ask them to collaborate on general questions such as:

- *How could this assessment have been better?*

- *What did you like about this assessment?*

Also, ask them specific questions about often-missed prompts:

- *This question was missed by numerous students. Even if you got it right, why do you think this prompt was problematic?*

Asking kids to help you improve involves humility on your part, but you'll learn a lot and your students will respect you for including them. They'll give you great advice that will help you improve future assessments and instructions. Best of all, you'll probably become an even better teacher.

WHAT YOU CAN DO TOMORROW

- **Create a unit learning target list.** Provide this list to students. Prompt them with specific questions about this list and consider their input when you build the assessment.

- **Formulate a revision template.** Decide on your revision policies and then work out the logistics of how you can implement your plan.

- **Craft post-assessment student prompts.** Tap into the wonderful primary sources that are your students. They'll have great advice on how you can help future learners.

Assessment has outstanding engagement potential. Follow these three steps and improve assessment performance, engage students in the process, and hopefully reduce anxiety.

CREATE CLARITY

THE PROBLEM: MANY STUDENTS DON'T KNOW HOW TO PARTICIPATE

I F A STUDENT actively participates, they must be engaged—right? I've been guilty of perpetuating this generalization. Back in the day, when I led classroom discussions or issued classroom prompts, I lavished praise on the enthusiastic participants. I'd think, *Those kids are with me.* But a lot of students weren't with me, and that was a problem. I knew my cadre of collaborators was not large enough. I wanted more students to enthusiastically put up their hands and more to engage in my lesson.

One obstacle was my perspective. I'm an extrovert. Uninhibited expression is in my DNA. Many of my students who were active contributors were probably wired the same. I didn't understand why some of my more reserved kids didn't just jump in and start yakking. While I intellectually knew that participation might be more difficult for reserved students, I finally paid enough homage to this phenomenon and knew I had to make changes to facilitate more engagement.

My early efforts at achieving these goals were fruitful. I placed greater emphasis on making any activity I issued, and any whole-class prompt I verbalized, as engaging and relevant as possible. I worked with students outside of class to make sure my prompts were hitting the mark. This was a good start. I also became cognizant of whom I was calling on.

I began working on the subtle and complex process of learning to coax participation out of less-engaged students through more intentional and empathetic questioning techniques. This was a game-changer. I learned that many students who I thought were not engaged actually were. When I created the right atmosphere for them to participate, they did, and their contributions were solid. But then, I discovered the secret sauce. And that's what this Hack is about.

THE HACK: CREATE A SELF-ASSESSMENT TOOL THAT SIGNALS TO STUDENTS HOW TO PARTICIPATE

If you've read one of my previous engagement books, listened to my podcast, or been a student in my class for more than a week, you know I'm a big fan of classroom discussion. An energetic and passionate classroom discussion is intoxicating. My class discussions became truly bacchanalian once I began employing this simple tactic that guides kids to be more participatory. If students have a self-assessment in front of them during a lesson, they can use it as a roadmap for successful participation. I ask students to use an online form (see a sample in Image 136.1) during a class discussion and then complete and submit it afterward.

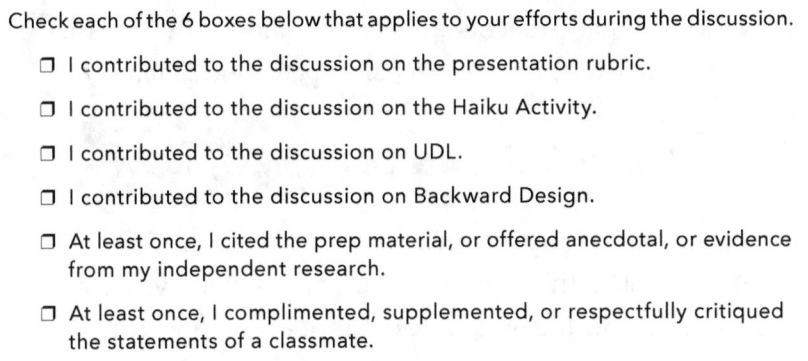

Check each of the 6 boxes below that applies to your efforts during the discussion.

❏ I contributed to the discussion on the presentation rubric.

❏ I contributed to the discussion on the Haiku Activity.

❏ I contributed to the discussion on UDL.

❏ I contributed to the discussion on Backward Design.

❏ At least once, I cited the prep material, or offered anecdotal, or evidence from my independent research.

❏ At least once, I complimented, supplemented, or respectfully critiqued the statements of a classmate.

Image 136.1: Students complete this online form to self-check their efforts.

If you didn't get all the points on the participation section, compose a narrative below on what you wish you would've said. It may also be that we ran out of time. Regardless, express yourself below for full credit.

Long answer text

Image 136.2: Students can compose a narrative on their missed opportunities.

What I've noticed about employing this tactic is that students frequently reference the self-assessment during the activity. I can sense them thinking, *Oh wow. I think he's ready to start asking about Universal Design for Learning. I better say something about the Haiku Activity.* This is positive, but students shouldn't feel pressured. The second form (see Image 136.2) displays the option for students to still get full credit by composing a narrative on any missed opportunity. You may have some introverts whose written narratives at the end of the self-assessment are long as they aim to compensate for short verbal narratives during the discussion. Over time, try to entice those lengthy narrative composers to be a bit more vocal.

This self-assessment tactic can also be utilized in group work, games, and simulations. It can even be used as a tool to enhance classroom citizenship. You can use it with kindergartners and graduate students and all students in between. Show kids how they can succeed, and they'll be inclined to participate more often.

WHAT YOU CAN DO TOMORROW

- **Create an engaging prompt.** Working with an idea is essential to this process. With some help, you may be able to do this with a topic that some find dull. Conscript some student helpers and bounce ideas off colleagues.

- **Be cognizant of non-participants.** Make a list of the students you'd like to see participate more. I walk into class each day with a plan: *Today, I'm going to try and get more participation out of these three students.* Sometimes my plans fall flat, but having this daily objective has been helpful.

- **Build a self-assessment.** This self-assessment can be electronic (a form) or physical (one sheet of paper). Ask for specific actions to help guide kids. An example is: "At least once I cited the preparation resources." Also, include a way for students to contribute an idea if they missed an opportunity. They can compose a narrative describing what they would've said if they had the opportunity or if they'd taken the initiative.

Some students want to participate, but they're not sure how. A well-crafted self-assessment can liberate such kids. They'll love feeling a part of things.

LOOK FLY ON FRIDAY

THE PROBLEM: MANY TEACHERS MISS SUBTLE WAYS TO ENGAGE STUDENTS

RIGHT AROUND MY fortieth birthday, I shaved my head. My follicles had been migrating for years. It was depressing. I had an old friend who was also hair-challenged, and he took the shaving plunge before me. The first time I saw his pristine shaved dome, I thought, *He looks great*. I asked him about it. His words were inspirational, "Be bald. Be free!" The second I got home that night, out came the razor.

My wife thought I looked good, which was most important, but I was also impressed with the compliments I got from students in class the next day. When I committed this sane act of recognition, I had no clue how it would impact my students. That's because I hadn't considered how closely kids monitor their teachers. Never underestimate your impact. In this case, they endorsed my decision. I heard:

- *I'm so glad you did that!*
- *That's really trendy!*
- *You look younger!*
- *You have a nice-shaped head!* (By far, my favorite comment)

I left class that day feeling great about the way I looked. It reminded me of when I used to coach football. One year, our head coach purchased new uniforms. The players donned them for the first time, and we assembled for picture day. Our kids looked great. We knew it, and they knew it. One of our audacious players looked at me and said:

"Coach Sturtevant—when I look good, I play good!"

I loved that. My new mantra is:

"When I look good, I teach good."

THE HACK: SET A GREAT EXAMPLE FOR YOUR STUDENTS BY OCCASIONALLY DRESSING UP

I enjoy a good jeans day like the next man, but there is something about occasionally putting on the dog. I'm not talking about wearing a stiff and uncomfortable outfit. I want you to consider an outfit that is contemporary, professional, and comfortable. Remember, you'll need to move around a lot—at least, I hope you move around a lot when you teach.

I currently have classes on Monday, Wednesday, and Friday. Fridays are, by their nature, celebratory. So this year, I decided that on Fridays, I step it up. Here's my typical Friday getup:

1. A buttoned-down dress shirt

2. A pair of dark, well-fitting jeans

3. A nice pair of black shoes and a matching belt

4. And one of my three blazers (navy, charcoal, and khaki)

This is an exceptionally comfortable ensemble. I'm wearing jeans, for crying out loud, so don't accuse me of being too fancy. But each time I sport a variation of this template, I also accessorize with one crucial piece—the pocket square. See one of mine in Image 137.

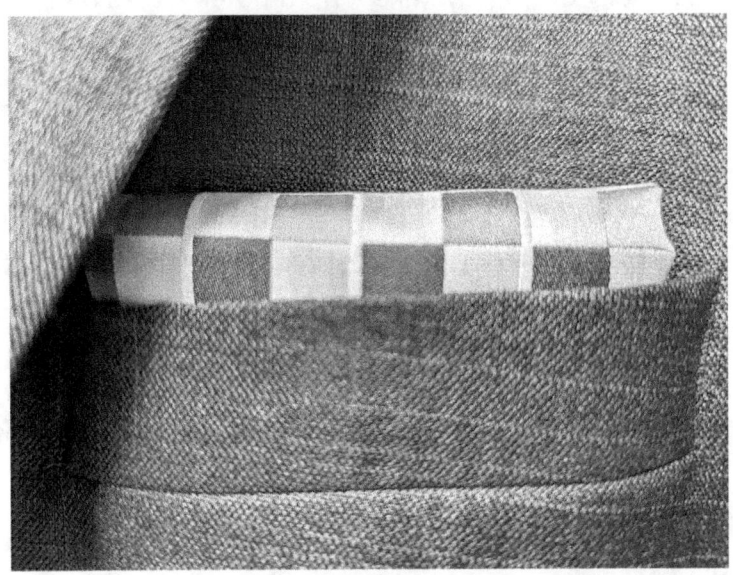

Image 137: My pocket square peeks out from my sport coat pocket.

The first Friday I wore this to class, my students, no pun intended, were all over it like a cheap suit. They loved the pocket square. Now, they're offended if I don't include one. I heard comments that first day similar to the ones I received when I first shaved my head. But one comment resonated deeply:

"Sturtevant, you're looking fly!"

So now I have a great moniker for those days when I dress up and a wonderful title for this Hack.

WHAT YOU CAN DO TOMORROW

- **Plan an outfit and an unveiling.** You want to look nice, but you want to be comfortable. If you dress professionally every day, take it up a notch occasionally. Also, decide when you'll unveil the new you. A more casual day, like a Friday, might be a great choice.

- **Prepare for inquiries.** If you dress differently, people will notice. Your students might not say a word, and that's okay. They'll still notice, and they'll still be curious (engaged). After you've worn an attention-getting outfit a few times, some extroverted kid won't be able to stand it anymore and will probably speak up and ask questions. This will provide you with a marvelous teachable moment. You may also get some snarky comments from sarcastic colleagues, such as "Who are you trying to impress?" Simply reply, "My students."

To some, this Hack may seem silly. Don't be hasty in dismissing this idea. You can bond with kids because of a compliment they've bestowed based on what you're wearing. And, although not every lesson you teach can be ultra-engaging, if you set a tremendous example, you may become fascinating and fill in those gaps.

138

PROMOTE BRAND AMBASSADORS

THE PROBLEM: ADULTS ARE TOO NEGATIVE ABOUT SOCIAL MEDIA

SOCIAL MEDIA PUTS incredible pressure on young people. Granted, you can inventory some positive results, but the impact has been a net negative. Your kids, however, are obsessed with their phones. And, dear reader, so are you, and so am I. Social media is not going anywhere. I post on social media, and I bet you do too. As educators, we might as well harness this incredible phenomenon for good.

Recently, I listened to a fascinating episode of the *On Point* podcast from NPR. "Inside the Lives of Social Media Influencers" is an engrossing window into a world that a number of your kids would probably like to inhabit. Perhaps if you have older students, you might challenge them to listen. This life is a lot less glamorous than one would think. It's lonely, it's exceptionally difficult to earn a living doing it, and it can be dangerous. When you put yourself out there, as these influencers do, you become exposed and vulnerable.

But let's be honest; there have always been media influencers promoting products. In the 1950s, tobacco companies ironically hired star athletes to promote cigarettes. What's happening today is nothing new, but it is different. Today's social media influencers promote every kind of product imaginable, and they create and then distribute volumes of content virtually independently. They become brand ambassadors in modern parlance. Brand ambassadors must excel in these skills:

- creative messaging

- technology platforms

- monitoring engagement

- artistic design

Being able to learn and repeatedly use these skills can land someone a great job. What if we use the brand ambassador motif as a powerful learning opportunity?

THE HACK: CHALLENGE STUDENTS TO PROMOTE A FUTURE LEARNING TARGET

Brand ambassadors promote a product, and the brand then compensates them. In this Hack, your students will promote one of your upcoming learning targets. How or if you compensate them is up to you. They'll create a social media-like post. It can be a captivating image created on Photoshop or Canva accompanied by a provocative caption. It can be a short MP4 video. Unlike social media, however, these posts are not for the world. Ask students to post them in a designated and protected area like your district's learning management system, or keep them contained to a small space like a Padlet bulletin board. These posts will be great hooks when it's the designated learning target's turn to shine.

Social media posts have a narrow engagement window. Scrollers on TikTok, Instagram, or Twitter are an impatient lot. One must engage them quickly, or they'll move on. Maintaining brevity while engaging deeply will be a supreme higher-level-thinking challenge for your kids.

This Hack is powerful because it leverages positive trade-offs of a problematic entity like social media. If they're successful, your students will also be promoting your future lesson plans in an epic fashion.

WHAT YOU CAN DO TOMORROW

- **Listen to the *On Point* podcast.** It's fascinating, and you'll get ideas about how to conduct this Hack. If you have older students, consider inviting them to listen too. You can also create a highly engaging lesson based just on the episode I mentioned at the beginning of this Hack.

- **Compile a list of future learning targets.** Brand ambassadors can choose between complex targets like "I can compare and contrast Cubism and Impressionism" and simplistic targets like "I can describe weathering." Regardless of what they choose, they're responsible for promoting this target till it goes viral at your school.

- **Compose a prompt.** Make certain that students understand their mission is to promote your learning target. Decide the parameters in terms of text length, video length, and image use or creation.

- **Create a display venue.** This is an important issue, and you may need your district tech guru to help solve it. I love the convenience and the appearance of a Padlet, but that might not work for you.

Your students no doubt follow folks on social media. They hold these figures in high regard and try to emulate them. They'll enjoy this challenge of trying to influence their classmates.

STOP CROSS-EXAMINING YOUR STUDENTS

THE PROBLEM: TEACHERS ASK TOO MANY LEADING QUESTIONS

MANY YEARS AGO, I was asked to assist with our school's Mock Trial team. On the first day of practice, I learned the difference between open-ended and leading questions. Lawyers ask open-ended questions to friendly witnesses:

What happened on the night of the 14th?

Such prompts allow a witness to tell a story, be expansive, and elaborate. Lawyers ask unfriendly witnesses leading questions, which often call for yes or no responses:

On the night of the 14th, you went to the movies—correct?

Such prompts funnel opposing witnesses into binary choices.

On that first day of practice, I was struck by how I behaved similarly to a trial lawyer in my classroom. I asked students a lot of leading questions. And even my open-ended questions were not open enough. I vowed to make my classroom less like a mock trial. Leading questions are not engaging!

THE HACK: ASK STUDENTS TRULY OPEN-ENDED QUESTIONS

The power of such questions became apparent when I was asked one. An education professor from a local university was observing my class. After the lesson, she prompted me:

> *I love the cultural climate in your room. How did you create this?*

This was a wonderful open-ended question that I had no idea how to answer. The question haunted me. That's what great open-ended questions do. Within a year, her rather innocent-seeming question inspired me to author my first book, *You've Gotta Connect*. My book answers her question. That book would not exist if it weren't for that question. Think of how such questions can enrich your students.

After my mock trial observation and the transformational question from my classroom visitor, I conducted a miraculous experiment.

What would happen if, on a regular basis, I ask students to take a simple everyday item and then associate it with a topic we are studying in World Civilization?

The next day, this engaging journey began. But first, a little background to the story. I like to look nice and put effort into my daily ensemble, and students frequently give me kudos for my daily getup. On the first day of my experiment, I named my outfit based on the unit we were navigating. I wore a green shirt and khaki pants, with a prominent red pen peeking out of my shirt pocket. We were studying the Battle of Tours, which took place in Central France in 732 CE. This is one of the most significant battles in history. If the outcome had been different, Europe and North America could be Muslim today. I glanced down at my outfit and up at my students, then asked a solid open-ended question:

My outfit today is called the Battle of Tours. Can anyone tell me why?

My students broke into groups. They loved this question, and their ensuing speculations were wonderful. They came up with creative motivations that I hadn't even dreamed of. After some joyous flailing and a number of leading hints on my part, some students started to hit paydirt:

- The green shirt represents the European biome.

- The khaki pants represent the deserts of North Africa.

- The green shirt is on top, north of the khaki pants on the bottom south.

- The red pen in the pocket in the middle of the green shirt represents the battle location.

The next day, I challenged my students to produce a name for my outfit, which had to be tied to the unit on Islam. They struggled. A few students eventually came up with loose but acceptable submissions. Then I remembered how I struggled when the visiting professor put me on the witness stand. When you ask students open-ended questions, you must give them time to create.

WHAT YOU CAN DO TOMORROW

- **Arrange kids in small groups.** These groups can be random or contrived.
- **Give each group a common object.** A coffee mug or a stapler are good examples.

- **Ask them to describe how this thing represents a concept you're studying.** Give them twenty-four hours to come up with something brilliant.

This is a steep creative challenge. It may be supremely frustrating for students. But it represents a wonderful, low-stakes, higher-level-thinking prompt that kids will enjoy.

INSERT YOUR TALKING HEAD

THE PROBLEM: MANY TEACHERS ARE RELUCTANT TO PRODUCE VIDEOS

WHENEVER I WANT to learn how to do anything, I go to YouTube. I've learned how to change a bicycle tire, install a tile backsplash, wire a lamp, and even pour concrete. I'll bet you've been schooled by YouTube too.

YouTube is the world's most successful flipped classroom. You learn about an idea and then attempt to apply it. With each example I just mentioned, I had to rewatch portions of the videos when I would get stumped in the application process. This is another magical learning empowerment attribute of a flipped presentation. In each case, I ended up successfully implementing what YouTube had taught me. My sense of achievement was powerful.

Unfortunately and understandably, educators in the wake of COVID seem down on virtual learning options. This is totally understandable. We all got sick of trying to create impactful and engaging virtual lessons during those bleak endless months. Whether educators like virtual learning or not is irrelevant. It's here to stay. The answer for you is to not make the walls of your classroom impenetrable. Parents and students will demand access to learning whether your school offers it or not. Virtual learning has currency. And video presentations are a key aspect of this type of instruction. You might as well get really good at making engaging videos.

THE HACK: CREATE A FIVE-MINUTE INSTRUCTIONAL VIDEO

If you're like many, you might not know how to create a video. It's not nearly as hard as you think. Loom is a wonderful tool. You create a slide presentation, hit record, and then start yakking. You have the option to insert your talking head. I strongly encourage you to do so. You want your kids to know that it's you who made this video, that you made it for them, and that your friendly face is in the video to prove it. Don't worry if you don't have an appearance that would land you a role on *The Bachelor*. I certainly don't. But please let them see you. Your presence will add a lot to student engagement. Image 140 shows my talking head in a Loom video.

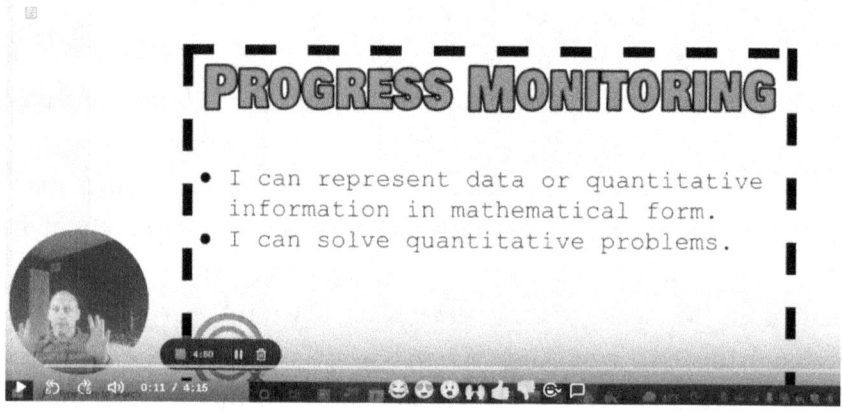

Image 140: My talking head in a video helps me bond with students.

Drastically reduce the amount of text on the slides of your video. Your talking head is a lot more engaging than trying to read text. If you want to include provocative or beautiful images on your slides, that is a plus.

It's important to keep your videos short. When I search YouTube to learn how to remove a screw with stripped threads, I look for the short videos. If your video is longer than five minutes, consider chunking it into two.

And finally, you can always film yourself with your phone doing an activity. That's the template for most of YouTube's instructional videos. Your students will be charmed to see you in your natural habitat.

WHAT YOU CAN DO TOMORROW

- **Pick a topic.** Your first video doesn't have to be engaging. I recently recorded one that explained to students the field experience process. It was helpful to my students and didn't burn class time with me explaining a straightforward topic. Get comfortable with a low-stakes topic like that, and then build your production skills from there.

- **Create a video.** You can use the camera on your phone or the video creation tool on the Loom platform, Screencastify, or your LMS (if it has a video tool). Don't hesitate to ask for help from your local tech guru.

- **Assess learning.** Just because you produce an awesome video does not mean that students will watch it. Create a formative assessment to accompany your video to check for learning and make certain they watched.

- **Instruct students to leave a comment.** This is how you can prime the collaboration pump.

Watching a video is the modern world's default way to learn how to do anything. This phenomenon is not going away. Stay relevant and learn to make engaging videos.

141

LEVERAGE A BIT OF SELF-DEPRECATION

THE PROBLEM: TEACHERS ARE AFRAID TO LOOK VULNERABLE

BEING AROUND A self-promoter is a drag. What self-promoters don't understand is that their boasting makes them appear needy and demonstrates a profound insecurity. You certainly don't want to be a self-promoter around students. Instead, humbly sprinkle in small portions of self-deprecation.

I capitalized on a self-deprecation opportunity on my first day as a teacher. It's all pretty fuzzy because it was a long time ago, but I vividly remember an incident in the parking lot right after school. This was in the days before the internet. That's good because if this had been captured and posted, it would've gone viral. Back in the day, if you wanted to study geography, you looked at a map or explored a globe. After that first day, I took a globe home to study. My hands were full that afternoon exiting

> *It's helpful to show some vulnerability— particularly to your insecure students.*

the building while lugging a large globe, my coaching attire in a bag, and two textbooks. I was pretty loaded down but also amped after my first day of teaching.

Absent-mindedly, I placed the globe on top of my car and unlocked the door with my free hand. I plopped into the driver's seat and unloaded my cargo, forgetting that the globe was still resting on top of the car. I started the car, backed out of my parking space, and then navigated halfway across the parking lot before the globe rolled off and careened across the blacktop. Many students in and around the parking lot witnessed this scene and howled with laughter. A crucial decision presented itself: emerge from my car sternly and glare at my tormentors while retrieving my dented globe, or get out and laugh at myself and shrug my shoulders and smile while gathering my poor damaged globe. I made the right choice. I even joked about it in class the next day, and it helped me bond with the kids who were unfamiliar with my gaffe. My rookie year was wonderful, and that incident helped break the ice.

THE HACK: TELL A SELF-DEPRECATING STORY

Here are two of mine that I tell students as a wonderful way to connect with them through the commonality of human blunders.

- When I was young and single, an attractive local woman asked me on a date. I was surprised and elated but then deflated when she picked me up and took me to an Amway presentation! Her advances were not romantically inspired. I only told this story after I moved to a new community.

- One day after school, I searched high and low for my car keys. Colleagues, custodians, administrators, and even students joined the search. I called my wife and asked her to come and pick me up. Ten minutes later, I realized that I hadn't looked in my pocket. It took me a long time to live this one down.

WHAT YOU CAN DO TOMORROW

- **Make a list of ways in which your students may feel inadequate.** My story of the date was designed to help students who face relationship troubles. My key story was designed to help any kid who feels stupid. When your kids see how you've survived *devastations*, it will help them learn to cope with theirs.

- **Search your memory banks.** Once you come up with your list, pluck an example from your past when things did not go according to plan. I'm sure everyone has an epic relationship fail story.

- **Don't overdo it.** You don't want to become an object of derision. If you self-deprecate too much, you'll appear pathetic. But sprinkle in a little here and there, and it will endear you to your kids.

You've achieved a lot more than your students have. You've graduated from college and landed a teaching job. You've become an expert on the subject that you're teaching them. Plus, you're an adult. Even if they don't always seem to respect you, they probably do. It's helpful to show some vulnerability—particularly to your insecure students.

FORM HOOK PRODUCTION TEAMS

THE PROBLEM: IT'S HARD TO CREATE GOOD LESSON HOOKS

HACK 67 IN *Hacking Engagement Again* calls on educators to "Dangle a Dilemma." This Hack promotes powerful lesson hooks, an engaging way to grab students' attention before the lesson, and it provides readers with a solid template for crafting them. However, you teach a lot of lessons, and coming up with so many great hooks is a challenge. Perhaps your students can help.

A great hook captivates student interest and primes their intellectual pumps for the lesson. Two elements must be present:

1. A great hook is engaging.

2. A great hook is relevant.

These two ingredients are elusive. I've created impactful lesson hooks, and I've created some duds. It's disappointing when some hooks fall flat. If you're over the age of twenty-three, you might make some miscalculations. Don't beat yourself up; it's natural and appropriate to have some separation between you and your students. The good news is that when it comes to creating epic hooks, you have dozens of primary sources seated right in front of you every morning. And these young folks are experts on youth relevancy. Go ahead and tap this remarkable resource.

THE HACK: CHALLENGE STUDENTS TO PRODUCE RELEVANT HOOKS

A recurring theme in this book is for educators to relinquish more control to students and collaborate with kids in the pursuit of deep learning. When you delegate to kids, they feel empowered and assume ownership—an awesome development, for sure.

You'll need to spend some verbiage explaining to students what a lesson hook even is. One option is to provide a humorous example. Years ago, a friend of mine shared a wonderful experience involving his then-twelve-year-old son. The young man called for a five-minute meeting with his parents and was elusive as to the topic. The parents gathered on the couch at the designated time. On the coffee table in front of them was the family laptop open to a colorful PowerPoint. The son then went through an impressive presentation he created to demonstrate the growing importance of technology in education. After he hooked his parents, he closed his pitch and proposed that the only Christmas present he needed or wanted that year was an expensive laptop. It totally worked! You can probably think of a similar story, or you're welcome to parrot mine.

Challenge your kids to speculate about why hooks are important and how they might use them outside of class. Have they ever softened up their parents? Promote hooks just like you want hooks to promote your lessons.

You can absolutely mandate that every student be part of the Hook Production Team. You can also make participation voluntary or allow for one-person teams. Not every student has to do every prompt. Even if you have a small number of voluntary Hook Production Teams, these students will probably be motivated to produce outstanding ideas. All of your students will benefit from a great hook regardless of whether they helped produce it.

WHAT YOU CAN DO TOMORROW

- **Make a list of upcoming learning targets.** Your list can include lessons that were engaging in the past and ones where you had difficulty.

- **Ask for volunteers.** Being part of a Hook Creation Team should be fun. It'll be even more so if such teams are voluntary. Hopefully, if your engagement pioneers are successful, more students will take the Hook Team plunge. Regardless of how many participants you entice, you'll likely end up with some great hooks in needed locations, which is a wonderful accomplishment.

- **Create a Hook Production Team calendar.** Consider spreading out the student-created hooks over the semester. Even if you have just three production teams, you can still build anticipation: "In just one short month, we'll get hooked by Maria's awesome creation team!"

- **Provide a prompt.** Give the team clear direction, but make it spartan: "Choose an upcoming learning target from this list, and create a hook for this lesson that will be engaging to your classmates and relevant to someone your age. Make certain the entire hook can be delivered in five minutes."

Student Hook Production Teams can make your life easier. And the hooks they create have the potential to be even more relevant and engaging to their contemporaries. This also represents another wonderful high-level-thinking challenge for your kids.

143

ENGAGE ALL FIVE SENSES

THE PROBLEM: MOST LESSONS DON'T LEAVE A LASTING IMPACT

CCASIONALLY, ONE OF my five senses will be engaged, and then I experience a powerful memory from my youth. I know it's the same for you. Here are a few of my sense triggers:

- When I smell the exhaust from a bus, I remember turning five in the Philippines. My family accompanied my father there for his sabbatical year. I don't have precise memories of that year, with one pungent exception. I distinctly remember the sweet smell of bus exhaust in congested Manila.

- On frigid Ohio winter mornings, I think about waking up for elementary school. I'd grab a blanket and lie by the heating register. I'd pull the blanket over me and the register and create a hot air bubble—instant euphoria.

- Whenever I hear a cicada, it takes me back to the haunting chorus I first heard at age four when the seventeen-year brood invaded my hometown.

- Whenever I hear a song by the Beatles, I reminisce about being captivated by the black-and-blue image on the *Meet the Beatles* album cover when I was three. It was my older sister's birthday present.

- And finally, a powerful negative example from when I was very young. My mom made me a peanut butter and jelly sandwich with a knife that apparently had onion residue on it. I nearly vomited and cannot stand the taste of onions to this day.

These things happened a long time ago, but their impact is still powerful. Wouldn't it be cool if our lessons had a similar shelf life? Perhaps we need to get our students' five senses involved.

THE HACK: ENTICE STUDENTS TO REPRESENT AN IMPORTANT CONCEPT VIA ONE OF THEIR FIVE SENSES

Asking students to demonstrate an idea in an unusual and unanticipated way is higher-level-thinking nirvana. This prompt also has longevity potential. Once students start to sense an idea, it has a great chance of sticking with them.

It's important to select great concept candidates by choosing complex ideas, such as:

- Math: probability

- Social Studies: the French Revolution

- Science: the Ice Age

- English Language Arts: any novel

- Health: fitness

- Elementary: being a good citizen

Ask your students to apply the five senses to the concept. This prompt will be a supreme challenge for many students, so it's appropriate to make it collaborative. You can have a group for each sense (Feel Group, Sound Group, Taste Group, Smell Group, Sight Group). Give each group expressive freedom. How they demonstrate a sense is up to them. They can do a skit, a presentation, or an audience participation (like a taste or smell test). Assign students a concept and then ask these questions of the appropriate group:

1. How does the concept feel?

2. How does the concept sound?

3. How does the concept taste?

4. How does the concept smell?

5. How does the concept look?

Give students the freedom to produce an incredible presentation. It won't be easy to represent complex ideas in this fashion.

WHAT YOU CAN DO TOMORROW

- **Formulate sensory groups.** You may have some brave individuals who want to tackle this prompt by themselves. By all means, let them go for it. But most students will find this directive challenging. Create groups and guide them to focus on just one sense. Allow kids to collaborate.

- **Pick the perfect concept.** Representing a complex concept in an abstract way involves really understanding that concept. Make this prompt count. Pick a concept that is essential to learning in your curriculum.

- **Create the prompt.** Keep your prompt simple. Assign a group a sense, provide the concept they are to represent, and give them ample latitude on how they can demonstrate their product.

Ideally, this lesson will cause your students to think and wonder about your lesson half a century later.

SCAMPER THROUGH YOUR NEXT EVALUATION

THE PROBLEM: TEACHERS ARE AFRAID TO BE VULNERABLE WITH EVALUATORS

VIVIDLY REMEMBER THE anxiety I experienced before, during, and after my first teacher evaluation. My principal could've non-renewed me for any host of reasons. Fortunately, he was pleased with my efforts and saw potential. He gave me clear improvement directives, and I tried to act on his suggestions. You may be wondering where this Hack is going. Bear with me.

As I matured as an educator, my confidence grew, but I found myself displaying my strengths while I was being observed. For example, during observations, I worked harder to:

- Solicit student participation

- Unleash student creativity

- Create an engaging presentation

- Facilitate enthusiastic group work

My evaluations were outstanding. But for long stretches of my career, I was in a holding pattern in terms of professional growth. My students paid the price for this willful stagnation.

THE HACK: DEVELOP A SELF-INITIATED GROWTH GOAL WITH YOUR EVALUATOR

The last portion of my K–12 teaching career was a magical epoch of professional growth. By that time, I'd achieved the confidence to be vulnerable and ask colleagues for help. This book, however, is about student engagement, not professional development. Yet, your weaknesses as a teacher stand in the way of student engagement. Consider addressing those weaknesses. I can say for certain that my growth enriched my students.

When you've taught for as long as I have, it's difficult to generate yearly professional goals. It was during such a September goal-setting conference with my principal, near the end of my K–12 teaching career, that I decided to be vulnerable. I had an *I need to get better* epiphany.

Personalization is a concept I have always endorsed, but I wasn't good at doing it. I expressed those concerns to my principal and concluded with this zinger: "Can you help me get better?" I thought the man was going to embrace me! I'm so glad I asked the question. He was resourceful. He connected me to the district instructional coach, and she reached out and encouraged me to try the SCAMPER Method. Dr. Rafiq Elmansy outlines this method in the online resource titled "A Guide to the SCAMPER Technique for Creative Thinking." Here's what this acronym represents:

- Substitute

- Combine

- Adapt

- Modify

- Put to another use

- Eliminate

- Reverse

You can give kids a concept and ask them to apply a letter from the SCAMPER acronym. I loved it.

My prompt was for students to evaluate an image of nonviolent protest. Each group was to make a stop-motion video from a slide-show presentation. I arranged my roster based on their nine-weeks grade average. I created nine groups of three. My lowest-grade-average group didn't have to transform their slide presentation into a stop-motion video, but they had to choose one directive, or letter, from the SCAMPER acronym and transform their nonviolent protest image. My three top-grade-average groups were also required to apply the SCAMPER method along with creating the stop-motion video. The groups in the middle were to create the video, but they did not have to apply the SCAMPER method.

On evaluation day, both my principal and the instructional coach came to observe. They focused on the group with the low class average and the groups that were at the top of the grade book.

At my post-observation conference, both the coach and my principal were jubilant. They were excited to relay the comments they overheard from the groups where they focused. They reported that the group with the low class average expressed confidence and relief in the lesson. The observers heard students say, "We can do this!" They also recounted how members of the top group were relieved that I didn't give them a busywork challenge but instead stoked their creativity.

My students benefited because this prompt was tailored to student learning needs. It engaged kids at all levels. My principal felt great because he successfully developed me. I got a wonderful evaluation. Please consider approaching your principal and asking for help.

WHAT YOU CAN DO TOMORROW

- **Consider exploring a weakness with your evaluator.** Only you can decide if this is the right move based on your working relationship with your principal. It takes chutzpah, but the potential payoffs are huge. Your administrator probably has a clear idea of where you need to grow. It'll probably impress her that you're showing up in a humble fashion and asking for help.

- **Solicit resources.** Asking your evaluator for a resource entices them to invest in your development. They become a member of your team, committed to your success.

- **Take a brave step.** Put your growth on display during your next observation. Please remember that your principal wants to see you succeed, and she's invested in your growth.

If you choose, you can make this time of your life be your magical epoch of professional growth. Your engagement and that of your students will soar.

EMBRACE ANONYMITY

THE PROBLEM: MANY STUDENTS ARE RELUCTANT TO SHARE THEIR IDEAS

THIS POWER OF anonymity is often underestimated. Early in my career, I once asked students a loaded question. I was hoping the prompt would ignite a passionate class discussion. Instead, the students nervously looked around at one another. No one took the bait. I was disappointed to learn that kids can be reluctant to express their ideas if there is a chance of negative social repercussions.

Another early teaching experience was also instructive. We were traversing a complex lesson. At the conclusion of class, I asked if anyone had any questions and was greeted with silence. I felt great about that until I assessed. They collectively didn't understand my lesson and were hesitant to display their lack of mastery when I prompted them to ask questions.

THE HACK: EMPOWER STUDENTS TO EXPRESS THEMSELVES ANONYMOUSLY

Tech platforms that empower students to post an idea or ask a question in a public, legible, and anonymous way are powerful. The old-school method of placing a sticky note on a poster board is okay, but it has serious limitations. Many notes are hard to read. The writing can be small and sloppy, and you have to walk up close to them to read them. And, you can see who posts what, so anonymity is lost. Anonymous posting encourages kids to be authentic, and the posts are displayed in a large font size so that everyone can read them on the screen from any place in the room. Many tools are available for anonymous student expression, but here are my favorites:

- Padlet

- Google Forms

- Plickers

- Google Jamboard (A wonderful student shared this tool with me.)

- IdeaBoardz

With each of these tools, students can express an opinion or ask a question incognito. When the potential for social stigma is reduced, authenticity soars. These tools liberate kids. They can communicate what they think, and they can ask questions without fear. You can prompt every student to signal you about confusing aspects of the lesson. If you get a number of redundant questions, you just administered an important formative assessment that identified a hole in your instruction.

I'd like to single out and praise the Plickers tool. While it's different from the others in that students cannot compose and then post narratives or questions, it's an excellent choice for young students or those who don't have phones. Give each student a half sheet of paper with a symbol on it. Then prompt kids with a multiple-choice template. Students rotate the symbol to represent their responses. The teacher then scans their symbols with her phone, and the results appear on the screen. I've used it with graduate students, and it never fails to impress.

My final encouragement for anonymous student responses is purely speculative. Study reserved students when you utilize anonymous posting platforms. You may notice a new level of engagement among these kids. I've observed them responding in animated fashions and then focusing on the screen to see their classmates' submissions. It's almost like I can hear their self-talk, "Wow. I guess I'm not the only one who feels that way." Or "I'm so glad I'm not the only one with that question."

WHAT YOU CAN DO TOMORROW

- **Investigate anonymous expression tools.** The list of tools in this Hack is not exhaustive. These are the ones that I've used successfully. If my description of Plickers stoked your interest, but you still cannot visualize it, merely go online and search for a tutorial.

- **Decide on a prompt.** This should be a provocative question or an attempt to get kids to express a lack of understanding. Anonymous expression tools can also be used to survey student opinions, such as, "Should we have the assessment on Friday or Monday?"

Asking students provocative questions is important. Allowing them to respond anonymously can lead to greater participation and more authenticity.

TEASE OUT RELEVANCY

THE PROBLEM: EDUCATORS OFTEN IMPOSE THEIR INTERPRETATIONS OF CONCEPTS ONTO STUDENTS

EVERY TIME AN educator takes on teaching a new class, they have to dig into the state learning standards, the syllabus, the text, and perhaps even interrogate the previous teacher about how they did it. Ultimately, *they* have to make sense of the course before they can teach it.

Your students do their own version of this, too, probably with every lesson you teach. This is Constructivist Learning. Here's a definition from the University of Buffalo:

> *Constructivism is the theory that says learners construct knowledge rather than just passively take in information. As people experience the world and reflect upon those experiences, they build their own representations and incorporate new information into their pre-existing knowledge (schemas).*

Ultimately, Constructivist Learning is all about relevance. And relevance is a crucial engagement ingredient. Too often, educators seem to forget that in order for kids to embrace a concept, they have to relate to it.

THE HACK: LEVERAGE STUDENTS' REAL-WORLD EXPERIENCES

Educators must prepare for any course or lesson with a constructivist disposition. An idea simply must first make sense to us before we can teach it. For an idea to make sense, we often apply our experiential filters. Unfortunately, we don't encourage kids to do this enough. Let's change this dynamic.

A great hook often promotes relevancy, but you can infuse it throughout the lesson, not just as an opener. A great way to consistently prime the relevancy pump is to frequently ask questions like the one articulated on the slide in Image 146. This slide came from my Education class.

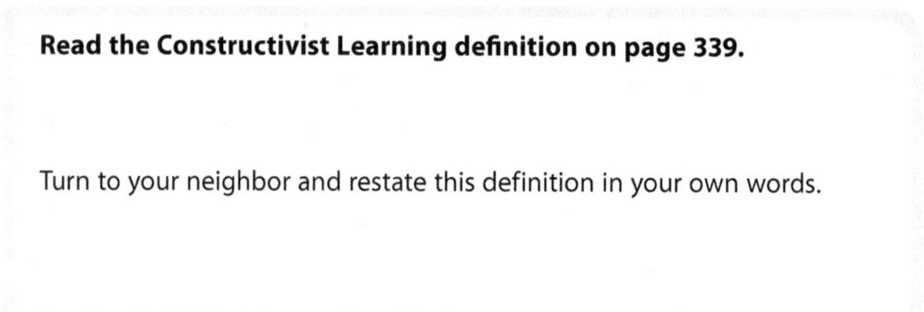

Read the Constructivist Learning definition on page 339.

Turn to your neighbor and restate this definition in your own words.

Image 146: Keep the topic relevant by asking students a question.

Please use this clarifying tactic with any important concepts. Such prompts set you up for awesome follow-up questions:

- Who had a personal definition similar to a neighbor's?

- You agreed that your definitions were similar, but that means they must have also been slightly different. How was yours different? What's your theory on why this difference exists?

- Who heard something totally unexpected from their neighbor?

- Did your neighbor's definition influence the way you think about the concept?

Another wonderful constructivist exercise is to employ a Venn diagram. On one side of the diagram, list descriptors of a concept, and on the other side, write a student's potential relatable life experiences. One can even challenge students to expand their life experiences to include possible future events or even life goals. It'll be challenging for students to populate the overlapping area of the diagram, but give them time, and they can do it. This real estate represents instant relevancy—how this concept and the student's life coexist now or perhaps in the future.

You can even challenge students to build constructivist models demonstrating academic concepts at work in their lives. Kids can create flow charts, presentations, artifacts, songs, performances, impact studies, and even research papers. This can be done in any subject and with any grade level. Here are some provocative prompts:

- Evolution: Describe a time when you fundamentally changed. What caused it?

- Ratios: Find a ratio that worries you.

- Persuasive writing: Write about something you read that influenced a decision.

- Economic trade-offs: What's been your most difficult decision? How did you resolve it?

- Elementary civics: What is your favorite rule? Why do you like this rule so much?

WHAT YOU CAN DO TOMORROW

- **Craft a *Define in your own words* slide.** This tactic is simple and powerful. Use it whenever you introduce a new concept.

- **Ask kids to build a model of an idea.** These can be graphic organizers or any student creation. Give them freedom, but ask that they tie the concept to their lives.

- **Create constructivist prompts.** Directives like the ones just mentioned will create instant engagement. Students will instinctively apply their personal experience filters. This often evokes profound understanding as well as engagement.

Teachers are ultimately constructivists. The only way we can teach a concept is if we understand it. This typically entails some constructivist filtering. Encourage your students to do the same.

EMPATHETICALLY EXPOSE BIAS

THE PROBLEM: PEOPLE DON'T REALIZE THEY'RE BIASED

B E SUSPICIOUS OF anyone who claims they aren't prejudiced, they're color blind, or they treat everyone the same regardless of how they look, where they're from, what or if they worship, or whom they love. They may truly believe this about themselves, but they're probably mistaken. This Hack will not only be revealing for your students but also has the potential to improve the future of your students and the world. When kids are unaware of their biases, they can miss wonderful opportunities like becoming friends with someone who's different. When kids are biased, it perpetuates injustices that desperately need to be eradicated.

THE HACK: EMPOWER STUDENTS TO FIND AND MANAGE THEIR BIASES

In introducing this challenge, it would be helpful to add some self-deprecation. Tell a story where you prejudged something inaccurately. This can be when you missed an opportunity or you had a nagging prejudice and then realized it was unfounded. Happily, my story falls into the latter category. You can also tell a story about when you judged someone unfairly. Be careful if you're going to use such an example. Students might miss the point of the story and view you as biased.

This is an example I've used for decades. It works well because students typically view me as loving teaching. This story surprises them. I majored in History and Political Science in college, and I thought about becoming a lawyer. However, the deeper I got into pre-law classes, the more boring the content became to me. In my senior year, I concluded that law school was not for me.

My next academic stop was to get a master's degree in history. During this foray, I decided to get my K–12 teaching license. This was my fallback. If I taught high school for a few years, that would be fine, and then I could go do something more grown-up. The thought of teaching K–12 in the long term did not appeal to me. I liked my high school teachers, but I didn't want to be them. Their jobs seemed kind of drab.

However, once I got my own class and taught the way I wanted to teach, I could not adequately express how at home I felt. This turned out to be the perfect job for me. Bias is like that. It holds you back and prevents you from experiencing great things. I'm so glad I didn't let my bias prevent me from becoming a teacher.

One of the most powerful tools to help students discover their biases is the *Harvard Implicit Bias Test*, which is available online. This impactful site can unveil negative feelings about race, religion, sexual orientation, and even body weight. When my kids dove into this resource, they were shocked—absolutely shocked—by what they learned. If you have elementary students, check out the Edutopia resource: "Teaching Young Children About Bias, Diversity, and Social Justice" by Jinnie Spiegler. You can learn more about the dangerous impacts of bias within education in the book *Hacking Deficit Thinking* by Byron McClure and Kelsie Reed.

Kids must become aware of their biases before they can take action. Importantly, their bias management mechanisms must be of their own creation. A solid first step is to arrange students in small groups and ask them to address the following issues:

- Have you ever been the victim of bias?
- Were you surprised by your results on the Implicit Bias Test?
- Can you share a time when you've been biased?
- What were you thinking when this happened?
- How could you have responded differently?
- What would it have taken for you to make a different choice?
- What is your plan moving forward?

Be prepared for some kids to totally clam up during these dialogues. That's okay! Some students might be embarrassed, and some might be defensive. But the fact that they are exposed to, and hopefully participating in, this dialogue is important.

At the conclusion of the group dialogue, encourage students to voluntarily share their ideas. These are loaded topics, and no one should be put on the spot.

WHAT YOU CAN DO TOMORROW

- **Take the Harvard Implicit Bias Test.** This free online resource is fascinating. You'll learn a lot about yourself. If you find that you are more biased than you realize, you have plenty of company—including your humble narrator. If you feel it appropriate, prompt your students to take the survey.

- **Designate a self-deprecating example.** It's so important not to come off as *holier than thou* to your kids. Hearing your biased example should help put them at ease.

- **Create a safe space for dialogue.** Put time into figuring out how you're going to group kids, what they're going to discuss, and if and how you'll have them share their ideas.

Two ideals are at work here. One, we want to promote a less-biased world. And two, we want our kids to take advantage of opportunities and not miss chances based on silly prejudices.

FOSTER FUNCTIONALITY

THE PROBLEM: MANY STUDENT GROUPS LACK DIRECTION

B EFORE MY WIFE was a principal, she was a guidance counselor. She loved this role, and she was darned productive at it. She also liked being part of a department—part of a team. But her collaboration with her fellow counselors was not without frustration. Penny likes direction, so when any group she's part of becomes aimless, she typically jumps in and assumes responsibility. "No one is clear in terms of who is supposed to handle what. I wish we had discrete job descriptions. So I'm just going to do it!" she'd often lament. I remembered her statements one day when I was frustrated by a student group's lack of productivity on a project. It dawned on me that maybe they, like my wife when she was a guidance counselor, needed more direction.

THE HACK: PROMOTE ROLES FOR GROUP MEMBERS

Unfortunately, many students have adverse reactions when they're informed that they will be placed in groups to perform a task. For decades, I've heard a variation of this complaint from frustrated students:

I hate group projects. I end up doing the work for slacker members, or my grade suffers because someone doesn't do their part.

I'll bet you've heard similar sentiments.

The University of Minnesota's Center for Education Innovation has produced an online resource titled "A Faculty Guide to Team Projects." One directive in this comprehensive guide stuck out:

Assigning roles is a good way to keep students accountable for team progress.

And there it is again: the demand for clear job descriptions.

Before you ask kids to work in groups, explain why you want them to. Give them a sales pitch. Here are some potential benefits:

- Learning to collaborate in a team is a wonderful and marketable skill.

- Joining classmates in a group can reduce isolation.

- Working in groups can be a lot of fun.

- A group frees you to talk and move instead of sitting quietly and listening.

- Groups bring diverse solutions to problems. You don't have to solve everything yourself.

- Groups can give you a sense of identity (I'm part of the Analogy Group!). Kids will laugh at this bullet.

- You might make a new friend or even find a future spouse. (Students will cringe while they laugh at this potential.)

- If you're trying to do everything, you cannot unleash your expertise.

- Groups can make you more productive.

These are powerful potentials that many group naysayers must acknowledge.

After your pep rally, let the kids vent. Brainstorm everything they hate about being funneled into group work. Here's where all the predictable venom will emerge. Prompt them to post their complaints visibly and perhaps anonymously, as I promoted in the *Embrace Anonymity* Hack. Once all the crabbiness is posted for the class to see, debrief students about the posts.

After they've gotten all the negativity out, and once you've created your groups, introduce the roles. This will be a wonderful transition. Typical group roles include:

- Facilitator

- Researcher

- Timekeeper

- Designer

- Materials manager

- Editor

Take a courageous step and prompt students to come up with the roles. Ask them what skills are important in relation to mastering your prompt. Once they create a list of skills, they can formulate roles. Also, prompt them to determine these crucial issues:

- How can they be assessed? Should there be a group grade or an individual assessment?

- How can they assign roles?

- How can they hold group members accountable?

Your students will love the clarity that comes from working out these issues before productivity begins. My wife would love to be in such a group.

WHAT YOU CAN DO TOMORROW

- **Read the "Faculty Guide to Team Projects"** resource that I assign to my Curriculum and Design students each semester.

- **Promote group work.** Express the importance of collaboration in many professions. Perhaps, share my "benefits of working in groups" pep rally bullets from earlier in this Hack.

- **Facilitate group roles.** This is the crucial part: empower students to organize, direct, and manage their groups.

This Hack is not a guaranteed fix for group work malaise, but it's definitely an antidote worth trying. It's so important for kids to learn how to collaborate and function in groups.

MOVE, PEOPLE!

THE PROBLEM: SEDENTARY KIDS LOSE FOCUS

AS THE PROUD grandparent of two rescue dogs, I do my share of dog-sitting when my human offspring go off galivanting. These two feisty female adolescent canines love their grandpa. I know that when I'm around *the girls*, sitting and watching television while they sit quietly and gaze at me lovingly is not an option. These young dogs want to move. And if I don't take them for walks, play fetch with them in the woods behind our house, or haul them to the dog park where they can erupt, there'll be hell to pay. I love these pups, and I try to treat them well by exercising them a bunch.

> *Get them moving. It's what young bodies want to do.*

Unfortunately, most human kids from kindergarten to graduation are treated with less consideration. We ask them to sit quietly and work, hour after hour. While your students probably won't be interested in going into the woods and playing fetch, I'll bet that they (even though they may complain about being too tired to get up) would benefit from moving around during transitions in your lesson.

THE HACK: INTRODUCE MOVEMENT DURING CLASS TRANSITIONS

I'll bet you do this for yourself. When I'm engaged in a taxing intellectual activity (like writing a book), I frequently take breaks. It's counterproductive to continue to try and focus. I'll stand up and stretch, think about something else, decide what I'll have for dinner, empty the dishwasher, go set the DVR to record a program, or do anything where I can move. Your class period has solid opportunities for you to entice students to do this, and these brief mobility forays offer opportunities for collaboration and relationship forging.

At the beginning of class, you can do the old icebreaker trick and have everyone relocate and greet those around them. Prompt them to share one thing they have planned for the weekend. Or, and this is powerful, make everyone go into the hall, and then you produce a paper that includes questions about the resource you assigned or review questions about the unit you're navigating. Each student gains entrance into class once they answer a question correctly— their entrance ticket. I always have easy questions or opinion questions for students who struggle. Everyone gets in!

Refrain from passing out anything non-confidential. This offers a wonderful movement break during the period. Students stand up and get their blood circulating as they amble up and get whatever it is that you're distributing. A humorous extension of this came from an interesting phenomenon I witnessed one day. I always have students march up and get stuff, but I noticed that a few slackers told friends, "Hey, snag one for me." The slackers remained firmly attached to their seats and waited for room service. The next day, I instituted *UPS Delivery Person for the Day*. I paired kids using the *Random Name Generator*. I then had them play *Rock, Paper, Scissors* with their new partner. Whoever won did not have to retrieve one handout for the entire period. The material would instead be promptly delivered by their vanquished partner.

As mentioned in many Hacks, I challenge students to collaborate daily. It's easy for them to do this with their neighbor while remaining in their seats. A more active method, and I'll argue a more engaging tactic, is to have kids stand and collaborate. Or, have them go meet their *UPS Delivery Person for the Day* and yak.

And out of the blue, in the middle of the period, on a random day when you sense a lull in engagement, create a random seating chart. I've had students shift to sit in alphabetical order by first name and then by middle name. I've had students look up how far their home address is from the classroom and then arrange themselves from closest to farthest. I've also done birthdays starting in January and ending in December. And, of course, there's always the *Random Name Generator.*

WHAT YOU CAN DO TOMORROW

- **Don't pass out anything.** Make them move to the front of the room to get it themselves.
- **Plan movement transitions.** At least once a period, get kids up and moving at a strategic juncture. Also, be cognizant of when engagement lags, and be prepared to act.
- **Create an entrance ticket.** This is a fun and easy way to start the day. It can also act as a powerful formative assessment.

Treat your students as well as you treat your cherished pet. Get them moving. It's what young bodies want to do.

START HAVING FUN AGAIN

THE PROBLEM: I DON'T HEAR MANY EDUCATORS SAY THEY LOVE TEACHING

THE SUBTITLE OF this book shouts, "50 New Ways to Make Learning Fun for All Students." That promotion sets this final Hack up perfectly because there's simply no way to maximize the potential of these ideas if you're not having fun. Remember the wonderful adage, *When Momma ain't happy, ain't nobody happy?* What applies domestically also applies to your classroom. Consider this rhetorical question: *Can the kids be happy if their teacher ain't happy?* I vote no. Your students reflect your moods. Being excited, enthusiastic, and positive about a lesson, a new tactic, or about teaching in general might not always translate into student engagement, but it certainly won't hurt.

THE HACK: CREATE AN ENGAGEMENT COHORT WITH COLLEAGUES

Think of this Hack as intrinsic professional development. That's PD you instigate because you're passionate about the topic. Cajole a few colleagues that you respect and trust into joining you once a week for an engagement throw-down. Each member of your little cohort will be responsible for bringing an idea and a question to each gathering.

The idea can be a lesson, a resource, or a tactic. It should be one that the messenger has tried or is about to try. The question can be asking for help with a lesson that has never resonated or for help coming up with a tech tool to make a learning activity more engaging. Shares aren't limited to lesson delivery. A *How to Improve Student Engagement* focus can also lead your cohort into the realms of classroom management and student-teacher relationships. Your gathering can be before school, after school, or outside of the building at a local coffeehouse. It can even be virtual. Choose the group members carefully; you absolutely want folks who will contribute. And, you can make this a secret society. This isn't a "let's sit around and complain about the principal" cohort. This is a "let's make teaching fun" cohort. Don't invite disruptors to join.

And finally, this group has great social potential. When you start working with colleagues in such a fashion, you typically grow closer to them. If you create a successful cohort, the positive feelings you experience will spill over into your classroom. If you get excited about a lesson, it will show. Students love having positive teachers, despite what they may claim. When you're engaged, the kids are engaged. Teachers who laugh at themselves for their positivity and crack a joke can often win over the cynics (without those students feeling like they're embarrassing themselves by buying in).

WHAT YOU CAN DO TOMORROW

- **Recruit a few like-minded colleagues.** You want folks who will contribute and participate. Those contributions may be more about bringing questions to the table than offering solutions. That's okay. Articulating problems takes courage, and such challenges, when attacked communally, can inspire creative solutions. If this cohort starts to feel like an obligation, bag it. No one wants to participate in an engagement cohort if the meetings are a drag. Learn from the experience and try another engagement cohort in the future.

- **Set a time limit.** A great way to maintain engagement is to introduce scarcity. In this case, scarcity means a limited number of gatherings. Run your cohort for one month or perhaps a nine-week grading period. If things go well, do another one next semester.

- **Create your first share.** Before you create this group, make sure you have a solid engagement idea for the first meeting. It wouldn't be smart to come empty-handed to the first meeting of a group that you created.

- **Designate drab lessons for an upgrade.** Besides coming to the first meeting with a solution, you'll also set a wonderful example if you come with a problem. Certainly, you have a boring lesson in your semester arsenal. Maybe your co-conspirators can help you transform it.

Often, teachers feel like professional development is done to us. An engagement cohort of trusted colleagues is the embodiment of intrinsic motivation. Wouldn't it be awesome to start having fun in the classroom again?

CONCLUSION

I N THE EARLY 2000s, the emerald ash borer slaughtered most of the stately ash trees in the northeastern US. We live on a large wooded lot in Ohio, smack dab in the middle of this invasion. Five of our massive ashes were victimized. They stood in our woods like abandoned skyscrapers. We're now down to just one of these beautiful and haunting relics. Seventy-two hours ago, three impressive corpses stood, but over the weekend, we experienced an impressive windstorm.

My wife and I watched the impacts of the powerful gusts from the safety of our backyard. The supple young trees swayed effortlessly. But we were eyeing our three towering ash artifacts. Sure enough, two bit the dust, literally, in dramatic fashion.

Our last standing deceased ash tree.

When my wife and I inspected the fallen trees the next morning, we both felt sad. These were marvelous specimens that, not long ago, we pointed to with pride. A tiny insidious bug followed by a strong gust of wind upended everything.

Many educators feel like they've been upended. They once knew their place, they knew their role, and they knew what to expect. Unlike the windstorm that blew through our woods last weekend, the challenges don't let up. Many teachers are hopping on the exit ramps. Fewer students are enrolling in teacher preparation programs. That's a tragedy because kids need us, and teaching is a wonderful job!

This is my thirty-eighth year in the classroom. I have experienced seasons of discontent, but I've always emerged stronger. Generally, what snapped me out of my funk was embracing new challenges. The Introduction of this book compared the Hacks to songs in a playlist. Maybe it's time for some new songs, a.k.a. new approaches. Hopefully, you have expanded your playlist, and you cannot wait to treat your students to wonderful new learning experiences.

My wife and I also noticed the survivors while we walked among the dead after the windstorm. We saw many young ash saplings that have replaced their ancestors, and we also observed resilient mature ashes. These trees are adaptable and vibrant. They will be around and thriving for a long time—just like you.

SNEAK PEEK

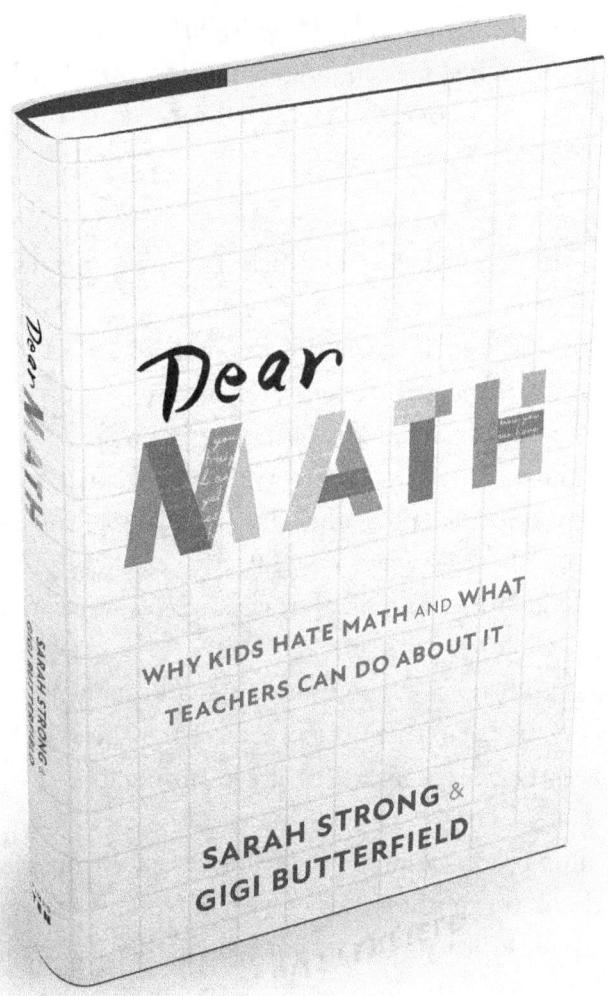

"Dear Math, I hate you; you make my clear skies feel gray.
In a world without you, I don't know what I would do,
though your own significance doesn't have to involve me.
I've never liked your certainty of 'right' or 'wrong' when it
ends up with just me unknowingly being dragged along."
—HAYLEY, TWELFTH GRADE

BECAUSE MATH INVOKES such strong emotions, often feelings associated with dislike and dread, I hope that we can hold space for these emotions and create activities where students can explicitly share their stories and unpack their feelings. Beyond caring about math and our students, we need to care about our math stories, particularly mathematical identities: how students see themselves as mathematicians and participate in mathematical spaces.

When he was president of the National Council of Teachers of Mathematics, Robert Berry stated, "Effective teachers affirm positive mathematical identities among all their students, especially students of color."

But why should we care about our students' mathematical identities? Can't we just teach them the processes they need to know?

The answer to this is, as we will see throughout this book, an emphatic "No."

The learning process inherently includes the development of identity. In his book on communities of learners, Étienne Wenger (1998) explains, "Because learning transforms who we are and what we can do, it is an experience of identity. It is not just an accumulation of skills and information but a process of becoming—to become a certain person or, conversely, to avoid becoming a certain person. Even the learning that we do entirely by ourselves contributes to making us into a specific kind of person. We accumulate skills and information, not in the abstract as ends in themselves, but in the service of an identity."

Students naturally form their own mathematical identities with or without our involvement. If we want students to engage in a better relationship with math, we need to guide them toward more positive mathematical identities. Recognizing how the unpleasant feelings they already have affect their identities is a strong first step.

> *"Dear Math, You are a cruel, heartless mistress."*
> —TONY, TWELFTH GRADE

Being able to share such strong emotions clearly creates the space to forge a path out of these emotions. Students may not even need advice or solutions for the problems they are experiencing; they may just periodically need to vent. Students come into our classrooms each day with a great variety of stories. If we do not create space for them to share their stories, then we are making it more difficult to help them create healthier relationships with math overall.

A LESS DREADFUL EXPERIENCE

Dear Math letters are a critical tool for understanding and overcoming dread for two related reasons. The first reason is that the letters give students a space to share their story, vent, and unpack the ways they have become the mathematician they are today. We can normalize experiences from the past, process them, and collectively make sense of a path forward.

The second reason comes from the teaching standpoint. If we don't ask, then we are designing curricula and making instructional decisions by relying on our assumptions from prior experiences, our own math experiences, or feedback we get from the loudest students.

I used to follow the ignorance-is-bliss concept, ignoring how my students already felt in favor of making my class as awesome as possible to help them love math. How wrong I was. I regularly assumed that the students were as ready to think about math as I was and that they were excited to learn it in the same ways that had excited me. I am reminded of Chimamanda Adichie's famous 2009 TED Talk entitled "The Danger of a Single Story."

In it, she states, "The single story creates stereotypes, and the problem with stereotypes is not that they are untrue but that they are incomplete. They make one story become the only story."

> *"Dear Math, I have always hated you; I can never do you. Sometimes I get the answer, but that's only on the better types of math. But I guess I need you because those 'Sometimes' are important in daily life. But I still hate you. I never look forward to doing you, I always look forward to finishing you and going on with my day."*
> —SAM, TENTH GRADE

Mathematics classrooms are easy spaces to become "one story." There is a math problem, there is a way to solve it, everyone tries it and does well or doesn't, and then we move on to the next problem. Dear Math letters hold space for and give voice to all the different math stories in the room. They allow healing for those with traumatic math stories and encourage the co-creation of stories that are whole and complete. Most importantly, they tell us things we wouldn't have known if we hadn't asked.

Every time I open a new Google Drive folder containing my students' Dear Math letters, my heart starts beating a little faster. I know some letters will reveal a dread for the subject that I must engage students in each day for an entire semester. I'll have to address their feelings in the ways that I teach. If the dread that students feel is connected to feeling rushed, we might try out fewer activities in our class that focus on speed. If their dread is connected to their grades, we might consider alternative grading activities or more equity-oriented assessment strategies.

But if I didn't ask, then I might delude myself into thinking that everyone was walking into my class ready to have a good time. Furthermore, I might unintentionally impose my own math story and identity markers onto my students, joining the oppressive figures I sought to dispel. Delusion and oppression are unhealthy starting places for a semester of work together.

BUY *DEAR MATH*

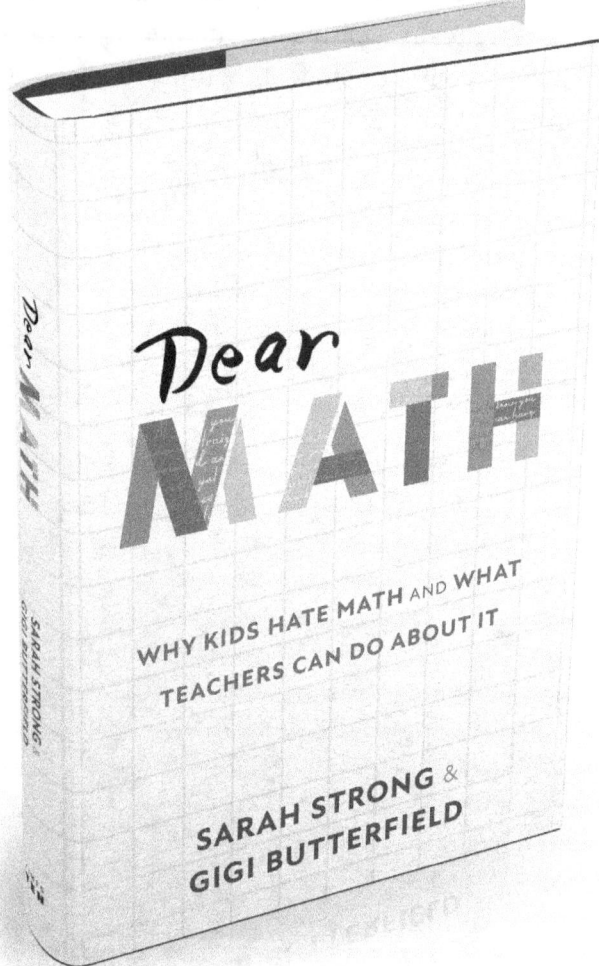

ABOUT THE AUTHOR

JAMES ALAN STURTEVANT is a thirty-eight-year veteran classroom teacher and author of *Hacking Engagement* (2016), *Hacking Engagement Again* (2017), and *Teaching in Magenta* (2020)—all published by Times 10 Publications. Jim is also the author of *You've Gotta Connect* (Incentive Publications, 2014). These books launched him into the national spotlight as an expert in rapport-building in education and engaging even the most reluctant learners.

Sturtevant's work has been featured in Huff Post, Edutopia, Principal Leadership, Ohio Schools Magazine, Talks With Teachers, Join Up Dots, and many other education resources.

MORE FROM TIMES 10 PUBLICATIONS

Browse all titles at 10Publications.com

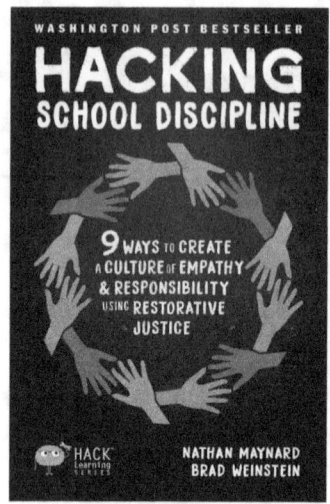

Hacking School Discipline

9 Ways to Create a Culture of Empathy & Responsibility Using Restorative Justice

By Nathan Maynard and Brad Weinstein

Reviewers proclaim this *Washington Post* Bestseller to be "maybe the most important book a teacher can read, a must for all educators, fabulous, a game changer!" Teachers and presenters Nathan Maynard and Brad Weinstein demonstrate how to eliminate punishment and build a culture of responsible students and independent learners in a book that will become your new blueprint for school discipline. Twenty-one straight months at #1 on Amazon, *Hacking School Discipline* is disrupting education like nothing we've seen in decades—maybe centuries.

Hacking Project Based Learning

10 Easy Steps to PBL and Inquiry in the Classroom

By Ross Cooper and Erin Murphy

As questions and mysteries around PBL and inquiry continue to swirl, experienced classroom teachers and school administrators Ross Cooper and Erin Murphy empower those intimidated by PBL to cry, "I can do this!" while providing added value for those who are already familiar with the process. *Hacking Project Based Learning* demystifies what PBL is all about with ten Hacks that construct a simple path that educators and students can easily follow to achieve success.

Browse all titles at 10Publications.com

Hacking Engagement
50 Tips & Tools to Engage Teachers and Learners Daily
By James Alan Sturtevant

If you're a teacher who appreciates quick ideas to engage your students, this is the book for you. *Hacking Engagement* provides fifty unique, exciting, and actionable tips and tools that you can apply right now. Try one of these amazing engagement strategies tomorrow: engage the enraged, create celebrity couple nicknames, hash out a hashtag, avoid the war on yoga pants, let your freak flag fly, become a proponent of the exponent, and transform your class into a focus group. Are you ready to engage?

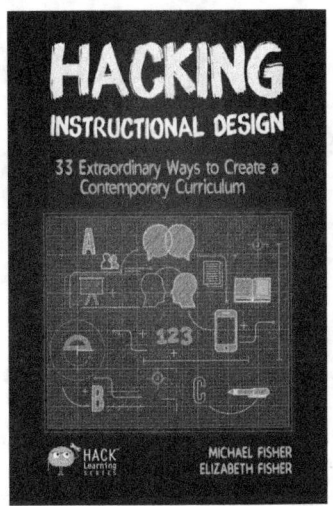

Hacking Instructional Design
33 Extraordinary Ways to Create a Contemporary Curriculum
By Michael Fisher and Elizabeth Fisher

Whether you want to make subtle changes to your instructional design or turn it on its head—*Hacking Instructional Design* provides a toolbox of options. Discover just-in-time tools to design, upgrade, or adapt your teaching strategies, lesson plans, and unit plans. These strategies offer you the power and permission to be the designer, not the recipient, of a contemporary curriculum. Students and teachers will benefit for years to come when you apply these engaging tools starting tomorrow.

Browse all titles at 10Publications.com

Teaching in Magenta
100 Paths to Joy and Well-being for You and Your Students
By James Alan Sturtevant; Illustrated by Lauren Barnes

What does it mean to teach in magenta? Magenta is bold, it's vibrant, and it holds noble qualities. *Teaching in Magenta* means creating magnificent days. It's a refreshing approach to teaching that puts your joy and well-being first so you can share those attributes with students. Veteran teacher and author James Sturtevant shares one hundred paths for living and teaching in an authentic, enthusiastic, and relevant way. Find renewed joy in teaching and become a refreshingly magenta teacher.

Hacking Classroom Management
10 Ideas To Help You Become the Type of Teacher They Make Movies About
By Mike Roberts

Learn the ten ideas you can use today to create the classroom any great movie teacher would love. Utah English Teacher of the Year and sought-after speaker Mike Roberts brings you quick and easy classroom management Hacks that will make your classroom the place to be for all your students. He shows you how to create an amazing learning environment that makes discipline, rules, and consequences obsolete, no matter if you're a new teacher or a thirty-year veteran teacher.

Browse all titles at 10Publications.com

RESOURCES FROM TIMES 10 PUBLICATIONS

10Publications.com

**Nurture your inner educator:
10publications.com/educatortype**

Podcasts:

hacklearningpodcast.com
jamesalansturtevant.com/podcast

On Twitter:

@10Publications
@HackMyLearning
#Times10News
#RealPBL
@LeadForward2
#LeadForward
#HackLearning
#HackingLeadership
#MakeWriting
#HackingQs
#HackingSchoolDiscipline
#LeadWithGrace
#HackingSchoolLibraries

All things Times 10:

10Publications.com

X10

TIMES 10 PUBLICATIONS provides practical solutions that busy educators can read today and use tomorrow. We bring you content from experienced teachers and leaders, and we share it through books, podcasts, webinars, articles, events, and ongoing conversations on social media. Our books and materials help turn practice into action. Stay in touch with us at 10Publications.com and follow our updates on Twitter @10Publications and #Times10News.

www.ingramcontent.com/pod-product-compliance
Lightning Source LLC
Chambersburg PA
CBHW061149120626
46546CB00005B/1983